Untamed Places

Adventures in Mountains,
Deserts, Jungles, Rivers, and Ruins

Norman Brown

SUNSTONE
PRESS

SANTA FE

Contents

*"The world is a book and those
who do not travel read only a page."*
— ST. AUGUSTINE

*(opposite) Temple towers bask in golden
light at Angkor Wat, Cambodia.*

Taj Mahal, from the palace where Shah Jahan was held captive; he had bankrupted the country building this monument to his dead queen.

Preface

As far back as I can remember, I loved geography. Every mountain, desert, and jungle exerted a pull on my young imagination, creating an itch to explore. As a young adult I lived in southern California and pursued this passion with backpacking and climbing in the High Sierra and trips into the Mojave Desert.

A fast-paced career in the corporate world took me all over the globe, but seldom with time to get beyond offices and meetings. I loved cities, yet deeply craved the beauty and challenge of the natural world. When I retired, my first project was to list earth's spectacular places, and since then I've been lucky enough to fulfill a lifetime of explorer's dreams, which are the basis of this book.

In addition to taking pictures, to my surprise, I began writing poetry. The clarity and compression it requires—along with rhythms, raw associations, and emotional leaps—helped me discover the essence of each experience.

Instead of organizing the book chronologically or by geography, I've divided it into four sections. First is an eclectic mix of necessary sights plucked from all over the world, a "sampler" of earth's garden of delights. Poems in the next section are grouped by different landforms—mountains, deserts, canyons, jungles, and savannas—each with the beauty and untamed power to affect us.

Then we delve into ruins of prior civilizations, often lingering as halfway houses between human striving and the natural world. The last section is arranged into poem sequences recounting an expedition to the most forbidding part of the Sahara, a month-long trek in the Himalayas, and a trip to the Outback in Australia and New Guinea. And finally, eight poems examine the merit of challenge, not just for travel, but for life itself. I invite you to join me and share these adventures.

Norman Brown
Santa Fe, New Mexico
January 2011

(opposite) Amazonian rainforest viewed from the top of a giant kapok tree in eastern Ecuador.

Acknowledgments

With enormous gratitude I thank all who have encouraged and supported me in this continuing adventure—family and friends, many intrepid guides, countless fellow wanderers. I offer the very deepest thanks to my wife, Lynn, our sons, Justin and Brendan, my oldest daughter and son, Pamela and Kendall, and other members of the extended family who provided important suggestions.

Especially I want to call attention to three persons without whose extensive help, this book would never have come into being:

Jack Foster—creative partner with whom I worked for many stimulating and successful years in the advertising world, a poet and author in his own right, who read, parsed, cajoled and inspired me to keep going as I explored the craft of poetry.

Carol Williamette—whom I met as a fellow adventurer crossing the Sahara, busy on her own book of African adventures, who patiently reviewed every poem, most of them many times, offering continued and invaluable insights.

Ken Brown—my oldest son, an Asian art history professor and author, who also studied every page and poem and who provided critical guidance on how best to frame this book.

One hundred sixty of the photographs are my own. The other thirty-five, as listed in the back, were taken by friends traveling with me or by professional photographers whose pictures better relate to particular poems. Many thanks to them as well for their permission to include their images.

(opposite) Victoria Falls, on the Zambezi River, divides Zambia from Zimbabwe.

Moments Full of Quiver

I want to stand struck
Where awe and exultation meet,
Journeyed into mountains, deserts, jungles,
Riding noble rivers, crossing far-flung seas,
Hearing ruins talk of old conspiracies.

I want to know our robust earth
Beyond the world set out on shelves,
Exploring things untamed,
Excited by extremes,
Facing hard realities of rough,
Each deeper measure of enough.

I want to soar on earth's abundance
Feeling edges washed in wild climes
And scratch a flake, a precious sliver,
Off the fleet intensity of time
And hold it for a moment, full of quiver,
Knowing that it's mine.

Introduction
Images and Poetry of Discovery

THE EYES OF THIS BOOK are focused on discovery. They range over the raw, physical world with feet on the ground, sweat on the brow, tingle in the spine. Human spirit deals with hard habitat. Whether a journey to one of earth's extremes or a place of gentle beauty, we explore both the experience of nature and the nature of experience.

Photographs are meant to climb out of their borders and interact with poetry placed alongside. Working together, they illuminate a third dimension often hidden below the surface of an image. Each page intends to capture the mood, or tell the inner story, fully embracing one of earth's spectacular places, people, or events.

Join me climbing Kilimanjaro, seeing Everest and K2 close up, or strung together with thousands of Japanese on an all-night pilgrimage to the top of Mount Fuji. Find yourself deep in the Amazonian jungle, or crossing the Sahara Desert with Tuaregs, starting in legendary Timbuktu. Retrace the Silk Road through China, examine ruins at Angkor Wat and Machu Picchu, probe Outback in Australia and Papua New Guinea, and meet the vibrant wildlife wonders of the Serengeti.

(opposite) "Big Daddy," earth's highest sand dune, rises more than a thousand feet above a bed of alabaster-colored sand in Namibia.

Elephants troop out beneath Mount Killmanjaro, Kenya, Africa.

Twenty Necessary Sights

. . . the great floodgates of the wonder-world swung open . . .
— HERMAN MELVILLE

Prologue

NONE OF THESE SIGHTS IS ESSENTIAL TO LIFE, yet each is a treasure, an image to be stored in our vault of significant memories that shine out over a lifetime. What are my twenty necessary sights?

Grouped here by subject, not in any rank order, consider: the sight of elephants below Mount Kilimanjaro, standing on the equator with glaciers on its crown, the velvet elegance and savage symmetry of a leopard at dusk, a million wildebeest pounding over the Serengeti, smelling moisture, or Galapagos Island creatures untamed, yet completely comfortable with us in their habitat   .

Gaze at Mount Everest, highest mountain on earth, the Matterhorn exerting its magnetic pull, and Fuji, a mountain turned into sacred pilgrimage. Feel the Sahara's vastness, its sand sculpted daily by the wind, and the Grand Canyon excavated by the Colorado River over billions of years.

Contemplate monuments heroic in scale, astonishing in their concepts—the Great Wall of China, pyramids in Egypt, temples at Angkor Wat, the ruins at Machu Picchu fusing Inca stonework onto forest peak. See the places that go with names long seared into our imagination: Timbuktu, Lhasa, Benares cradled in the the Ganges River, Dogon people dancing eight hundred years of animistic belief.

Watch Angel Falls leap from a lost world thousands of feet above the Venezuelan jungle; experience the Amazon River with discharge greater than the next ten rivers combined, organizing life for every living thing on half a continent.

Climbing Kilimanjaro

It rose above old legend and mystique,
A dream begun in tangled tropics,
Days of strange lobelia,
Eerie groundsel large as trees
Looming through the mist and clouds
That hovered over icy moors
Before they reared into the massive crown
Commanding distant sky, with
Blue-white glaciers hanging down
Like pendants on its majesty,
Indifferent to our scant reality.

Yet we continued up the flank
And measured it with footfalls,
Every step reliable,
Proportioned undeniable,
Connected to another and another . . .
And we caught that mountain unawares,
Surprised it by the force of our intent,
Seduced it with a trail of heartbeats
All dissolving into days,

Until the distance simply disappeared,
Vanished like a mist before the sun
And even that highest wall
Was finally undone, rolled over flat,
Handing us the glacier-guarded summit
Swaying slightly, so it seemed,
In the frozen moment of a dawn
That set us free beyond
The mere obsession dreamed.

Clouds that hung at 16,000 feet partially obscured the breech wall in front of us,
to be climbed the next morning. We reached the summit a day later at dawn.

Machu Picchu in the Twilight

Twilight settles on the cavities of heart
That beat within these ruins
Where cries of ancient sacrifice
Animate a soon-departed sun
And stimulate the moon
To slide its pewter
Softly onto suicidal slopes.

Beyond the chasm resting on
The Urubamba River coiled below,
Distant mountains kneel
Staring at this ridge
Waiting for a word, a whisper
Calling back to life that prior age

When Inca kings occupied their throne,
And the cold priestess of the moon,
Virgins of the sun, and gods
In golden bodies, bulging eyes obsidian,
Ruled each blazing day

Instead of hiding now in shadows
Where they slot their time-worn keys
And keep a careful watch
On those presumed to be asleep.

*Machu Picchu weaves a spell with all the force of lost culture
and irresistible topography.*

Leopard at Dusk

The silhouette was fluid
Poured liquid cool
Into unsettled night.

A forest flower wakened,
Dark beauty of its petals
Spotted furry on the perfect stalk
To roll a shiver
Down into the evening chill,

Tally distance, speed,
Divide by power applied,
Leap and strangle, kill.

Waiting for that impulse click,
Citrine eyes slit,
Window to the quick,
Exquisite raw machine incised lean,
Cross hairs set
Where craft and hunger meet
Savage, clean.

*This leopard makes her quiet observations as dusk settles
on the Okavango Delta in Botswana, Africa.*

Angkor

Trees exploit compliant sky.
Vines and creepers strangle walls
Within long-cloistered halls,
And prowl the corridors
To cast their greenish light
Where stone skin shed in places
Falls beneath enormous, reoccurring faces
Floating like full moons
Encased in towers
With odd, elliptic smiles
That half surrender eyes,
Yet seem to paralyze
The centuries.

Temples stand behind colossal moats
Arrayed in epic symmetry
And thrust their shapes
From grandly elevated stages
Full of passion peaked in other ages,
Walls astir with battles fought
In fixed relief
For galleries of gods
Beguiled by carved apsaras swaying
To a silent, ageless music playing.

The great temple complex at Angkor in Cambodia, built by Khmers a thousand years ago, is considered by many scholars to be the greatest architectural effort ever undertaken.

Conceived in faith and stone
To capture both eternity and space,
To help earth and heaven here embrace,
They struggle with
The sap and fiber flowing,
Roots feeding forward
Flexing muscles into cracks
To pry apart the seams,
While lichen unrelenting gleams.

They smolder through the swarming days,
Each temple reaching up in splendor
Focused on divinity,
But journeyed from a deep antiquity
And wedded to this jungle
Ardent in its purpose,
Feral in its hunger,
Every stone possessed and beaten,
Slowly being eaten.

One temple was left just as it was found, half recaptured by the jungle.

Honeyed Desert Dunes

Flirtatious dunes unwind and swirl
Like honey spooned to wind,
Its traceries upon their sand
Worn sheer as finest filigree
Worked lovingly by hand.

Their hearts stay firm and true,
But let the edges loosen up
To dance in undulating rhythms
For the pleasure of this land.

And in the fullness of late afternoon
Before these dunes slip on
Their flimsy gowns of night,
They drink their fill of setting sun
And beckon burnished gold,
Aroused and fresh again
While you and I grow old.

Sahara Desert near Chinguetti in Mauritania,
which was once described as "the ende of the worlde."

Angel Falls

Flowing softly through the ages,
Flowing from stark parapets
That clutch their strange remainders,
Gathered waters—
Rushed into this headlong plunge—
Fall through chiseled crenellations,
Splashing off each ledge,
Spreading out in mist and spray,
Swooning,
Losing all recall,
The waters simply fall,

Until that frantic reaching down
To feel a solid jungle floor,
Their breathlessness of drop
Burst into explosion,
Fraught into a fresh beginning,
Sundered into song
That weaves beneath the boughs
Gliding loose and free,
And with some luck,
To find that river, Orinoco,
And a distant, waiting sea.

*The world's highest falls drop a dizzying 3,212 uninterrupted feet in
southern Venezuela.*

The Amazon dominates half of South America. Even several of its tributaries have a discharge sufficient to rank among the world's ten mightiest rivers.

The Amazon: Imposing Order at the Edge of Complexity

Sultry attitudes of sky
Working for the sun
Exploit the soggy weave of wet,
Induce it up away, stored unseen,
Soon to shower down
And burst abundant green.

Excess seeps to pools
That sport a youthful readiness to grow,
Striplings turned to streams
Excited by their fluid force, and yet
They find themselves attracted
To some larger river's course:

The broad and black Rio Negro,
Deep and blue Xingu,
Madeira rushing rich and thick,
Each a prince of destiny,
A world unto itself,
Its being every thing become,

But seized into a grander sum,
Each drop conscripted,
Whirled into the service of
That true and only lord of all,
That ultimate phenomenon
Colossal River Amazon.

Straight Talk
in the Galapagos Islands

Blue Footed Boobies

"I can't believe that you prefer
Some other male to mate,
When you can see my courtship
Lovingly displayed for you!"

　"I'm sure you are sincere, my dear,
　And I appreciate
　Your feathers spread out true, but yes,
　It's best if you withdrew.

　"The nature of our kind is clear:
　We must perpetuate
　The color bred in feet, and his
　Are deeper, deeper blue."

One can't help but feel sorry for this male putting on a splendid display,
but look at those pale feet!

Our group followed the script. Unfortunately.

Giant Tortoises on Mount Alcedo

"My god, they must be dumb
To clamber up four thousand feet
Of bare volcanic habitat—
But take a look, here they come!"

"Arrive by boat at dawn, I've heard,
When it's still dark and cool,
To climb the barren seven miles
Before the sun turns absolutely cruel."

"That red-faced fellow there,
Just watch: the huffing, puffing idiot
Will barge right in,
Reach down and feel my shell,

Then take a picture, maybe two,
Before he looks into the smoke
And makes his tired little joke
That our volcano looks like hell."

"And, pronto, they'll begin to go,
No other choice of what to do,
But sizzle all the way back down
And know they could've, should've
Seen our cousins in the zoo."

Timing of the great wildebeest migration depends on when it rains in Tanzania and Kenya.

Reporting on the Wildebeest
Dispatches from the Front

Mass Movement Sighted

Our troops are on the move.
Thousands tramping over flattened grass
Arriving here in wavered lines
That steadily appear,
Droves of fresh reserves
Coming forward from the rear,
Arranged in loose assembly,
Told to stand at ease,
Eating when they please,
This army traveling on its stomach,
Filled with belch and grunt,
Marching on the Serengeti Plain,
Marching to the front.

Allies Join Forces

Our forces have been joined
By allies in the field,
Zebra personnel.
Their first platoons just arrived,
Integration and deployment
Yet to be contrived,
But how they strut, all set to go
In snappy uniforms
They're always proud to show.

Hard Maneuvers

Some observers scoff and say
Our army leaves a lot to be desired,
But we report
On discipline acquired:
They faced those waiting crocodiles,
Yet only briefly milled about
Before they hit the water
In courageous, mass profusion,
Eyes grown large, limbs thrashing
For diversionary confusion,
Plunging straight ahead, accepting losses,
Leaving many dead.

And just an hour ago,
They formed a giant circle side by side,
Staring beady-eyed,
Sentries posted closer, prudent care
To signal sooner any movement
From the lions lurking there.

General Staff Not Seen

We've not seen the general staff
But know they must be smart
To plan each grand, coordinated move,
Passing down commands,
A never-ending chain—
Removed, themselves, of course,
From all the blood and dust and danger
Marching on the Serengeti Plain.

But crocodiles are always ready, waiting at each river that must be crossed.

Dogon Dancers

Sacred caves and clustered dwellings
Climb the heavy-browed escarpment wall,
Where solid granaries,
Two stories tall,
Spread along the base
And squat on narrow ledges
Clinging to the broken edges.

Mud-built houses
Barely holding onto slopes,
Exude an aura upward into niches,
Honoring ancestors lodged above
With continuity of love
That calms and reaffirms the clan,
And clones eight hundred years
Of staunch belief in animal divinity
To fill this ark with fresh antiquity.

Dark-robed elders
Stand in solemn attitudes
Upon a square of leveled sand
Beside musicians, giant drums in hand,
Blowing wooden whistles,
Striking iron bells
To summon animistic gods
Floating in from all around,
Dancing masks that suddenly surround.

Men on lengthy stilts
Adorned in cowry shell and bead,
Breasts of baobob, step into the lead
Walking just like water birds,
Their mincing movements, every whim
A mimic of exquisite ladies
Loose and languorous of limb.

Wooden crosses leap and lunge,
Chase the swift gazelle,
And foxes, sly, turn away each eye
As shamans shake and sacrifices die.
Creatures gyrate, heave, and swell,
The whole procession rattles, sways
Alive on bright, expository days

And churns into illusion—
Circled dragon, whirling head
That swallows tail
While land expands and crusts
And rocks roar
And dappled figments float,
The dragon's tongue extended,
Flickered, curled
Tasting textures, raving textures
Of this world.

*The Dogon moved to this remote, nearly uninhabitable region south of the Sahara,
in what is now Mali, about six hundred years ago to avoid Muslim religion and slavery.*

This Great Wall

Behold this wall that springs
From Yellow Sea surf
To climb unending mountains,
Squirm through gorges,
Shimmer in recurrent waves
Across the Gobi like a snake
Intent to know the nap
Of all the westward-flowing land.

Ponder bone-deep nightmares
Filled with hard barbarians,
Terror shuddered deep
That tumbled millions into toil
To build this ever-lengthened wall
Commanded by imperial decrees
Through twenty Chinese dynasties.

Envision nightly fires
Blazing on ten thousand towers,
Signals sent in smoke
Across the Middle Kingdom space
Until they reached the Gate of Sighs,
That place of utter sadness
Where all order ended,

Where disfavored souls,
Sick and choked with fright,
Were walked through its portal into night
To face assorted demons
Sure to overwhelm,
Banished there beyond this wall
To lands that lay beyond the realm.

Built between the fifth century B.C. and the
sixteenth century, it extends nearly 4,000 miles.

Lhasa

Overbearing sun, club in hand,
Swings across the axis of each day
And smites the sky
In blinding, bellicose display.

People prostrate struggle forward,
Scrape and jerk for miles and months,
Intent to reach their holy city
Like an arrow aimed in faith,
But shot in blood and marrow.

Mountains keep the peaks aloof,
Their karma cold, unsullied
High above the hard, aggrieved plateau
Where pilgrims down below
Inch into Potala Palace,

Rising up in waves of raw emotion,
Surging currents of devotion,
Buddha glowing in the candlelight,
Each metamorphosis completed
In the ecstasy of sight.

This is a necessary sight for many pilgrims from all over Tibet, some crawling for weeks, semi-prostrate, to express their devotion.

Mount Everest From
Tengboche Monastery

Tibetan prayer spoken
Mani wheel spun
Sutra chanted
High inside the Himalayan world.

Crystal river
Flow denying time
Spruce and fir
The monastery here,

Sacred centered realm
Coupled to that peaked high
Supporting clouds
Above its matriarchal eye.

Stone disposed to stone
A day for now, but more somehow,
Eternal thrum
For this and every life to come.

This is the spiritual center of the Sherpa world. My poem honors the Buddhist guide who led us up to Everest.

The Matterhorn

Right there would be
The Matterhorn,
Just never mind the cloud
Obscuring all those attributes
With which it is endowed.

We crossed the ocean, traveled far
To see this peak of world renown,
To gaze upon its peerless sheer,
To marvel at those slopes careening off
The quintessential crown.

And here we wait,
Our eyes like lasers on the spot
The Matterhorn is fixed to be . . .
But it is not.

Here the bottom third of the mountain shows as a faint triangle just above spruce trees,
but even that could not be seen by the naked eye.

Good Morning, Fuji

Floating in perfection,
Self-absorbed among the clouds,
Serene in soft reflection
Lifting mist,
Fuji bared its soul
And we could not resist.

At dusk we found ourselves
To be three tiny drops
Drawn into a tide
Of pilgrims young and old,
Each with shining light
Glazing there in flecks of gold
A moving stairway
Climbing up the night.

The early hours went by
In gladdened expectation,
Buoyant camaraderie,
Elated crowds at huts
That offered food and rest,
Comforts edged into
The raw exertion
Of an odd, compulsive quest

But higher elevations
Brought ambitious winds
That launched thick clouds
Of biting cinder grit
And sharpened claws of cold
That turned our long ascent
Into a night
Of near-continuous torment.

We formed a human chain
Stretching out a mile,
Bodies partly numb,
In places single file,
Stumbling over loose debris,
The old volcano holding us
To some implacable decree.

In time, the whole procession
Shifted to slow motion
Cadenced to an unknown step,
Ahead somewhere
A person sick or deadly tired,
Who had become the weakest link—
Until, at last, the sky
Blossomed up in pink

While we, at steepest angles,
Fought the scouring wind
To reach the summit crown
And learn its only truth:
That everywhere was down
And curious night was gone,
Like us had struggled free
Between the streaks
Of Fuji's brilliant, blazing dawn.

Pyramid

Two million blocks of stone
Conceived in bold geometry
And heaped higher
Than the world had ever known

Were clad in brilliant white
To satisfy the sun,
Emblazon pharaoh's stature
And unprecedented might,

And set in upward symmetry
A walk to heaven that the gods proposed,
Leaving here a perfect crypt
To punctuate that history.

The mummy, stolen and exposed,
Suggests an afterlife gone wrong,
But even emptied of that opportunity
He struck this blow

For immortality,
Beside the Sphinx,
Enigmatically supposed.

Most scholars believe the Great Pyramid at Giza was completed in 2560 B.C. as a tomb for the pharaoh Khufu in the fourth Egyptian dynasty.

Timbuktu

Are you
That fabled city steeped in old
Impression, fortune's glory
Fixed and distant on Sahara sand,
Your antique mystery
Still branded on the desert breeze
And burning ends of history?

　　Or
Just this shrunken mummy
Laid to rest in sand,
Surrounded by old ghosts
Now buried in a buried land,
And casting spells so dry
Your withered wizardry
Entices only rare, eccentric souls
Who seek in vain
For temples, riches, and the sages
Now remaindered
To the yellowed pages
Of your past . . .

*Sankore Mosque is one of the few remnants in
this proud city that flourished four hundred years
ago in what is now Mali.*

Now called Varanasi, this is the oldest continuously lived-in city in the world.

River Ganges at Benares

Morning mist collects a cold dawn,
Obscures the sun,
Glazes River Ganges gray
And hides flames
Where piled bodies burn,
Where ardently devoted flow,
Descending worn embankment steps,
Spilling off the ghats.

Souls detach,
Seeking purity beyond our mortal chase
Busy with its seeds and
Soft-skinned fruit to follow
In a fractious, grand profusion,
Some to ripen,
Most to bruise and rot
In random, unresolved confusion.
Ganges bathes it all in certitude,
A sacred, soothing balm
Absorbing ashes of the dead
As well as twitching filaments of hope
That seem to float forever
In the comfort of its calm.

Late Light Falling
into Grand Canyon

It simmers in the late light,
Exhibitions of an excavated earth,
Elastic shadows reaching down
To drape their dark disparity, cathedrals
Rising up in violence and orange,

But walls all lose their grip.
Beauty blackens,
Subtext overtakes the sight,
Shivered into night,
Images in tow.

And still we stand and stare
Intent to tint some lingered tracing there,
Not seen, but predisposed to grow
Beyond mere sight, out past
The ether and the afterglow.

Hindu names given to many of the soaring cathedral shapes add to the canyon's mystical power.

The sun's first rays at Arches National Park, Utah

The Eloquence of Earth

"Nature does not hurry, yet everything is accomplished."
— LAO TZU

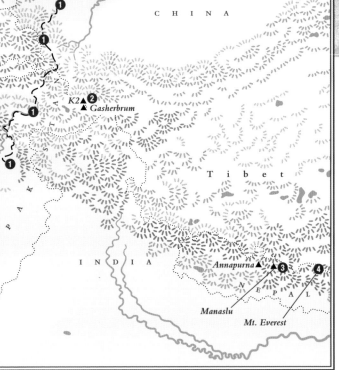

Slides on the Karakoram Highway require continuous repair and present major hazards to travelers.

The highway (1) lurches 600 miles from China into Pakistan. K2 (2) is a few miles to the east. Annapurna and Manaslu (3) and Everest (4) are a thousand miles to the east.

Mountains

I LOVE ALL OF EARTH'S LANDFORMS, but it seems to me that mountains make the boldest statement. My first extended trek was in Nepal to see Mount Everest. From the moment the small Twin Otter aircraft touched down on the ragged airstrip at Lukla to drop off a load of trekkers, I was over-the-top excited. Most of the group was young, but the guide and I were both in our mid-sixties and felt a strong kinship. He had been lead Sherpa on the first successful American ascent of Everest and said he was now "out to pasture," leading treks up to base camp. Being newly retired, my situation was similar. My Everest poem is set at the sacred center of the Sherpa world, and is dedicated to him.

Climbing Kilimanjaro was a journey of compelling inner discovery, as well as a physical adventure. And the all-night pilgrimage on Fuji ended up being more about the people than about mountaineering. In this section, the first three poems take us into the Karakoram range in northern Pakistan, the most dramatic on earth, after which we head to Torres del Paine in Patagonia, then conclude at what, to my eyes, are the most beautiful mountains—the Dolomite Alps in northern Italy.

The Karakoram Highway connects China to Pakistan. It crosses Khunjerab Pass and skirts five glaciers before careening down into the Hunza Valley, then sneaks through the most vertical stretch of land on earth before it finishes, threaded onto the nearly sheer walls of the Indus River gorge. You can share this experience, safely, in the poem that opens this celebration of mountains.

My second brush with the KKH, as it's known, was with three young men I call the Wild Bunch. We met at the Pakistani Airlines counter in New York, having signed up for a trek to see K2. Its height is second to Everest, but it is the connoisseur's favorite, as is the mind-bending trek up the Baltoro Glacier to see it. Our goal was a place called Concordia, an incomparable spot where half of earth's thirty highest peaks are located within a few miles.

As we ascended, many trekkers and climbers were coming down, all grumbling about the weather being socked in for several weeks. We crawled into our tents that first night at Concordia expecting another storm. But at 3:00 a.m. I woke up to shouts and, unzipping my tent flap, discovered the storm had miraculously blown away. Every peak stood out in the moonlight. Thereafter, we had three sunny, glorious days, rare in an area known for its extreme weather. We'll be everlastingly grateful for that good luck.

I sat up in my tent one night so filled with the beauty, so smitten by those peaks that I found myself writing poetry. Feelings poured out about the place and the human effort it took to get there. That was my first poem and since then, on adventures all over the world, I've combined poetic images and photos to get at the essence of an experience.

My desert hat helped with the extreme solar intensity at the start of our trek to reach the Baltoro Glacier and K2.

No Name Tower, center, and Great Trango, right, where it begins that awesome rise as the world's greatest nearly-vertical rock wall.

Paul Whistler with K2 behind him. He, Brad Nichols, and Kevin Hessee had just returned from a day hike to Gasherbrum I, while I relaxed happily at Concordia.

Mitre Peak stabbed the sky directly behind our campsite at Concordia. Our guide assured us its face was too steep to hold enough snow to pose an avalance threat.

Riders beneath a giant sand dune in the Pamirs, the first mountains encountered on the Karakoram Highway's tortuous journey from China to Pakistan.

The Karakoram Highway

What can be said about those things
Implausible, heroic madness,
Wild conception grown to grand design?
—To build this road
So begging for calamities,
In full denial of earth's realities.

Crawling out of cringing desert
Ancients knew as Turkestan,
The Karakoram Highway
Swallows dust of moldered caravans
And splits the rising loaves
Of soft-hued sand
And shinnies up an agitated land.

Corrugations bulk and buttress,
Massive peaks emerge,
The road arching ever higher,
Lofting to a heavenly plateau
That Marco Polo well described,
The road above the clouds,
Travelers funneled into caravan,
Khunjerab Pass, a snowy gate
That opens to the roof of Pakistan.

Abruptly there, at sixteen thousand feet,
The road submits to rough descent,
Careening off enormous shoulders,
Skirting glaciers,
Running gauntlets formed of falling rock,
Veering, sneering past the slides
Bombarding sheerest earthly mountainsides.

Battered, bruised, and torn,
And sometimes flung like hammered scrap
Into the bottom of a chasm—
Unlucky vehicles swept upside-down,
A terrifying final ride—
The road survives two wheels wide,

And, quickly, squads of men appear
Determined to restore,
Redraw this line on nature's face:
Delusion of a puppets' dance,
As if the problem's happenstance.

We walked over to inspect a vehicle knocked into the stream,
only its wheels above water.

Stretched and frayed
From binding China onto Pakistan,
The road arrives in Hunza,
Fabled kingdom full of gardens,
Medieval magic terraced into time,
Slopes that slip even when they climb.

Once again the road goes grim,
Evades Rakaposhi Peak
And creeps beneath that cold,
Misshapen Cyclops eye,
Nanga Parbat staring from the sky,

A run of easy miles,
A chance to brace and grip,
Before it falls into
That crimped and cloven
Nightmare world unfurled,
The Indus River gorge.

*Nanga Parbat looms in the distance, ninth highest peak in the world,
westernmost of the Himalayas where they crash into the Karakoram
in a colossal tectonic upheaval.*

The road just ragged ribbon
Pinned onto its precipice,
Clinging to the cleft,
Each traveler choked by fresh concern,
Stroking death at every hairpin turn.

Dark villages grown sullen
String themselves beyond our grasp,
Beyond our laws,
Trucks and travelers simply
Passing through, barely hanging on
Until the gorge begins to flatten out.
Six hundred miles of fantasy and doubt
Are quickly left behind,
Like purple oath thrown back
At indescribable terrain,

And the Karakoram Highway
Quietly slides down
And disappears
In heat haze of the Punjab plain.

*I've been on the walls of this gorge twice—once in daylight,
once at night. Darkness definitely has its rewards.*

The Baltoro Glacier and K2

The mighty Karakoram
Hurls peak after peak, stacks
Tower upon tower,
Flashing savage granite teeth
Like circled sharks
Full of fang and snag,
Spike and pike and pinnacle.

Eons, cross-examined, tell of
Grinding rivals, vast tectonic plates
That heaved excoriated masses upward
To be severed, sawed in half
By glaciers using frozen force
And birthing braided rivers
Underneath the ice and rock and snow.

Already driven into anarchy,
The surfaces are gripped each day
In tongs of penetrating freeze,
Then hammered on the anvil
Of a hard rock heat,

Which makes a place unparalleled,
That rattles at the crux
Of every keen explorer's goals,
That floods a mountain lover's dreams,
And was, for us,
The trek that pounded heartbeats pure.

We hiked those bouldered riverbeds
And edged along unconquered walls,
Skirting frozen tarns
That looked like slivered tin,
Defying—stare-for-stare—
The blinking blue-eyed crevasses
And doom-clad ice seracs.

We pushed beyond our limits of fatigue,
Remaining razor-wire-aware
Of shifting, aggravated ground,
But felt that tension lift away
Each time we raised a glance
Into the vast, incredible surround.

Some ice floes and seracs stand several stories tall,
while intersecting crevasses threaten from below.

We are on the dark snout at the lower end of the Baltoro Glacier.
Higher up it will be wrapped in snow.

We walked that godlike giant's face
Watching melodrama play
In theater of such astounding form and scale,
Beyond condition or control,
It shaped our days of slog and grapple
Into gape-jawed wonder
All enclosing and profound,

And led us to a treasure house,
An isolation called Concordia,
A sanctuary circled
And immutably icebound,
Where glaciers sweep the feet
Of mountain deities:
Broad Peak and Masherbrum,
Six summits forming Gasherbrum,
The sharpened edifice of Mitre Peak
Directly overhead.

And there upon its throne,
Surrounded, yet alone,
Appearing sovereign and severe,
We saw, and knew we'd finally seen,
The essence of all mountains

Raised to rightful, higher order,
Projected to its perfect prominence,
That massive angled ultimate—K2—
At home in this unrivaled place

Where mountains ride on ice beds
Driving chariots of snow
And reap the wind's feral cry
And call unbroken spirits here
To rise and storm the sky.

*Concordia is at the confluence of three glaciers and four of the world's
fourteen highest peaks (8,000 meters or more).*

K2, mountain of mountains, with late alpenglow lighting its 28,250-foot crown.

Concordia and the Moon

The moon came out, alert to flirt
In daring escapades of dark,
To dance in arms
Of dashing, virile peaks,
Each suitor clamoring for claim,
Flexing sharpened slants into
Their manliness of crown.

But she cavorted in between
Those swells of mountain prowess,
Nimble on her feet, at ease
Within the loosened cloak of night,

While beaming bright endearments
Down to us, seizing all our hearts,
Intent to dance us dizzy
In the music of the sight.

On the first night at Concordia, a worrisome storm blew away and moonlight danced down to circle our camp in silhouettes.

Patagonia

Five thousand miles of Andes end,
Caught running south
Past the Amazon's green glow,
Beyond Peruvian plateau,
Arrested here upon this farthest land
And raging in a final show of fury
Like some prehistoric beast,
Blades bristling on its back
Jabbing at the sky
Before it crawls away to die
In churning southern seas.

Scarcely memory of trees
Erased in older ages,
Glaciers run amok,
Their sheathing slabs of ice
Melted since to silver lakes
Beneath a wind that screeches, squalls,
Ranging free,
Grass alone staked out defiantly,

Though pierced by condors
Diving through the solitude and space
To finish picking clean
The helpless beauty carved into this place.

Torres del Paine Park at the bottom tip of Chile fills the eye with its look of sculpted, frozen loneliness.

Musings in the Dolomites

A Hero's Life

Mountains live a hero's life,
Grow up to be the strong and silent type,
A sheriff standing firm in any fight
With solid jut-jawed face
And heavy knuckled hand
To keep unruly land
Corralled within its proper space,
Then turn a gentle side,
All smile and crinkly eyes,
A quiet "shucks" if you point out
They also bolt in place the skies!

Inside Our Oyster Shell

In spite of those fine attributes
Some people feel that mountains rub
Like grains inside an oyster shell,
They force an end to meadowlands,
Place upper limits on the trees,
Then dwarf our tallest spires,
While forcing travel roundabout
Instead of where we please,
And when it's cold they'll frost a storm
With extra wind and icy whirls,

But, by the way, don't they string out
With all the elegance of pearls!

These mountains combine exquisitely chiseled features with the soft radiance of lush valleys.

Hikers returning from the three peaks (Tre Cime de Lavarado) a short distance north of Cortina d'Ampezzo in Italy.

Winds Blow

Boisterous winds patrol the sky
Jousting with intrusions there,
Enlisting other elements as well
To fight in that perpetual cabal
Against whatever stands too tall,
Intent to grind at peaks,
To pick at every elevated foe
Until it joins the mealy soil below!

Clouds Hang Loose

And yet, objectively, it's clouds
Not wind, that ought to be upset,
For they're at risk to snag and fall
Deflated from a rip or tear—
But they don't seem to care!
Just swallow up their pride
And then diffuse into another cloud
Or back into the air.

Sunbeams Act Shifty

Sunbeams are a different case.
Intercepted by a mountain's height,
They tend to flatten out and slide,
Take the opportunity to ride,
Pursue the easy path down slopes,
But in that bargain warmth goes glib,
Becomes mere surface shine,
Disappointing hopes!

The huge dunes encroaching on this slender oasis town even look hungry.

Desert and Canyons

WHILE MOUNTAINS MAY BE the most outspoken feature on earth, to me deserts and canyons are the most seductive. I had gotten a sense of the Sahara on vacations in Morocco and Egypt, but it was on a full-scale adventure trip to the western part of Mauritania that I came to love it. The poem "Desert Spaces" that opens this chapter celebrates the lyrical beauty of the landscape as well as my experiences with nomads on that first extensive desert journey.

A strip of desert along the coast of Namibia is the oldest on earth and the second driest, averaging only a quarter inch of rain per year. It also contains the highest sand dunes in the world. The bush pilot who took us there in 2003 held the record for climbing the tallest, called Big Daddy, which rises a scorching thousand feet and is the subject of my poem "Father of All Dunes." The pilot tried to better his record while I timed him from the bottom, but he missed by two minutes. Farther north, we'll look in on another otherworldly place known as the Skeleton Coast. Most mornings it is blanketed by fog that provides just enough moisture to keep a few plants and animals alive.

I've traveled to spectacular eroded lands on every continent—the flaming cliffs of the Gobi Desert, Wadi Rum in Jordan, the bizarre red center of Australia, but in my opinion the Colorado Plateau of the southwestern United States surpasses all others. Sprawling across four states, it was carved by the Colorado River and busy accomplices—the Green, the San Juan, and multiple lesser tributaries. Together with cycles of freeze and thaw, and the wind, they have created an awe-inspiring gallery of red rock canyons, striking buttes, and crumbling hoodoos that rise like ghostly effigies. Perhaps Edward Abbey best described it in an article that he wrote for the Museum of Northern Arizona in 1976: "When all we know about it is said and measured and

Berber nomads were unfailing in their hospitality, inviting us into their tents for tea, then passing a bowl of goat milk from person to person.

Tent Rocks: Weird pumice and tuff formations enclose a narrow slot canyon just forty-five minutes from my home in Santa Fe, New Mexico.

Time seems to stop, and it feels as if earth's layered strata are flowing past us on the Colorado River, rather than the other way around.

The Dogon people in Mali at the southern edge of the Sahara Desert in Africa and their predecessors, the ancient Tellem, carved houses into escarpment walls that are virtually identical to the cliff dwellings in the southwestern United States.

tabulated, there remains something in the soul of the place, the spirit of the whole, which cannot be fully assimilated by the human imagination."

Four poems included here are set on the Colorado Plateau. Three of these take place in national parks—Bryce Canyon, Arches, and Canyonlands—while the fourth stares into the phantasmagoric, almost nihilistic scene observed from Muley Point near Mexican Hat in southern Utah. Next, a sequence of nine poem vignettes takes us down the Colorado River through the Grand Canyon. These poems mix the excitement of running white-water rapids with the wonder of gazing up at ever-changing cliff walls and exploring side canyons, turquoise pools, and waterfalls—all of which present a grandeur that is simply unrivaled.

Mesa Verde housed thousands of ancestral Puebloans at Cliff Palace, shown here, and in other dwellings scattered throughout the area.

Only a quarter of the Sahara Desert is sand, but, oh, the beauty of dunes in splendid repose beside an oasis.

Desert Spaces

Sahara of a thousand faces,
Grave, expressive places
Etched in loose immensities of stone,
Chasms raggedly re-sewn,
Sand in pancake dollops poured
Across the blackened gravel beds,
Then baked into surrealistic scenes,
Dunes a carousel of serpentines
Fanned by palm fronds lifted high,
Their green composure orchestrating
Each oasis sigh,
While rough escarpment walls
Stake dividers in your fanciful mosaic.

Sing oh desert sing
Your desert songs to me:
Celebrate the Tuareg sword and poetry,
Their elegance with tea,
The caravans imprinted on your soul,
Camels channeled to a timeless sea,
Each nomad tent that fills its sails
To glide on gorgeous swells
That often run in parallels.

And whisper, desert, whisper lovingly
To all your little rippled creases
Carved in shore-less sand,
That live their spare eternity.

Those few sailors who made it to shore from a vessel that went down along this coast were not the lucky ones.

Desert Never Meant to Be

Intrepid currents leave Antarctica
And ruin every chance of rain,
Creating desert here, earth's oldest,
Most intense with pain.

Wet suppressed cannot get by,
Land erodes dumbfounded dry.
Split ends of desiccation swell
And hollow into dust,
Their throats too thick to cry,
While time turns rust
And reds in bitter rings
Beside an alkali so white
It blisters into bite.

Rag of what was leaf,
Lizard under rock,
The whole Namib a pan of powder
Sifted through the searing wind
That shapes and curves
Elongate walls of helpless sand
Where Spanish galleons
Broken long ago and lost at sea
Jag their jutting struts
On desert never meant to be.

Father of All Dunes

Stumps of dead acacia
Sacrificed beneath the sun
Raise their blackened arms
In homage to
The towering, lordly one.

He blazes apricot and orange
In rich imperial glow
Reigning high above the alabaster court
Receiving supplicants
A thousand scorching feet below.

Chains of sand corkscrew down
And make a shrill, unholy sound
As if each grain were tortured,
Stretched, and being ground
Upon some cruel rack—

Last confessions hurled back,
Offered to this sovereign of the sand,
This Grand Inquisitor,
The highest dune on earth, supreme
Atop his unbelieving land.

Heat rose in thermal waves and there was dead silence, a scene out of Dante's Inferno.

Colony at the Cape

No beach umbrellas, chairs, blankets,
Vendors hawking fizzy drinks,
No Nathan's Famous—
Hold the mustard, please!
Who needs a Boardwalk, souvenirs,
Or lotion, talk of burning sun,

Aren't we having fun?
No sign of sharks or whales,
Those nasty birds that dive
And carry off the young.
The tide is in with loads of fish
That swim beneath each wave.

What more could anybody crave?
Friends and family, flesh to press,
The happiness of crowds,
No nine to five
Nor politics with tired debates
About equality or greed.

We've got full opportunity to feed
And neither rich nor poor
And equal space to sleep at night
And mate . . . aye, now there's the rub,
If you're not master with a harem,
You better play your cards just right.

Cape Frio, at the northern end of the Skeleton Coast close to Angola, is known for this enormous seal colony,

Inland it's a moonscape with a few "adaptive" animals and eerie places where stones the size of grave markers were arranged in circles by Neolithic inhabitants of the area.

Empty Peeled

The feel of empty peeled
Opens out and spreads,
Vacancies inverted,
Nothingness asserted,
Old remains and grains
Curved away composed,
Deficiencies exposed—
This shimmer misted called
The Skeleton Coast,

Where odd mirage
Assumes the shape of oryx,
Tracks traverse a dune
Then shrug into giraffe,
And elephants
Roll defecated rounds
That come to rest beside old stones
Assembled by some band
Of prehistoric men
Who searched for silence in the wind
And substance in the sand.

The San Juan River is down there twisting in that labyrinth of its own making.

Null Hypothesis at Muley Point

An algorithm gone astray,
Equation warped, withered,
Earth deformed,
Vermilion sorrow turned absurd
On mutilated ground, roughage cheap,
Dorian Gray painted close and deep,
This parched, repeated crime,
With moldered music keeping time,
What earned the land this fate?

Water grinding ages,
Wind shearing loosened pages,
Silence gone off key
Where lullabies still lash both sand and stone
In mauve, prolonged, Cretaceous moan,
Consilience twisted inward out too late
For trilobites in hardened schools,
Shrimp alone
Alive in shrunken pools.

No more than river's rusted hull,
Nature's necessary cull?
Or earth impelled, off the track,
Spinning in the spiral of its null!

Incendiary

Dawn arrives
With schemes to overthrow
The sky.

Insurgent fuses
Lit in cracks of crumbled night
Fill with fresh incendiary intent,
Combust, then quickly flare
And conflagration blazes up
To torch the morning air

And sweep across
The stunned high desert plain
Where sentinels alone
Remain,
Charred, but still erect,
Valiant holding sway
To give us handles
For the coming rush of day.

*With a camera beside my sleeping bag, I had only to sit up and marvel
as dawn torched the sky.*

Hoodoos at Bryce Canyon are the unbelievable work of wind, water, and ice in continuous freeze-thaw.

Hoodoos at the Dance

Spires and columns cluster
Crowded into rows, arm-in-arm
And looking worn, creased
And torn, yet full of pride
Standing rigidly erect
As if in keen anticipation . . .
What do they expect?

Blushing in the light,
Their radiance effused into
A peach and alabaster sight,
Hordes of hoodoos
Wearing sunny, hopeful hues,
Caps set straight and smart,
Want just a chance
To dance away the blues . . .
When will the music start?

Fifty million years gone by
They've waited eagerly
To waltz and swing,
Twirl their partners do-si-do,
Be for once a moving thing
Instead of fragile and sublime,
Then spend their farewell years
In fanciful decline, slow dancing
To the beat of tertiary time.

Patience

Patience worked to virtue
Dry reward of time
Has no tribune
Has no rhyme

Shaped outside intent
A silent treasure shared
Less than solid
More than air

It arches out of both
Fragile favor
Briefly bared

Delicate Arch, 52 feet high, stands on a windswept ridge at Arches National Park in southern Utah. How much longer will it endure?

The Colorado River flows 277 miles from Lees Ferry to Lake Mead, tumbling over a rapid every 3 miles on average, presenting earth's grandest canyon in a geological pageant that cannot be imagined; it must be seen.

Down the Colorado River

Illusions Rising Sheer

Light and shadow rearrange the rock,
Forming intricate facades, illusions
Stacked in loose abstraction,
Dizzy dancers climbing sheer
Assembled by our multiplying eye
Into the checkered vision
Of a fitful butterfly.

Around the river's bend,
Red Wall Cavern
Spreads its clam-like lips apart,
A chamber filled with timeless sand
That mutes our footstep's fall,
While echoes of each voice
Ride the rim, but lose velocity
And disappear into
The eons' deep, insistent call.

Facing Cold-Eyed Killers

The Roaring Twenties and Sockdolager,
Hance Rapid and Horn Creek,
The vicious fury of Crystal Falls,
Cold-eyed killers lurking
In these narrowed canyon walls.
They boast of lives they've notched
On rocks and waterspouts,
And trigger every fusillade of shouts
Rising from the fling and spray
That flying, yes, deliver
Buoyant spirits whooping, roaring
Down the Colorado River.

Vishnu Schist

We pass the oldest folds
Of black and river-polished Vishnu schist,
Result of an explosive blast,
Recast and rounded for two billion years
Since that extravagance of birth.

The river acts attracted, yet repelled,
Controlled by some magnetic lure,
The schist seemingly alive,
Glistened like an alien stone,
The bone-core of an older earth.

The Hidden Realm

The sounds of water falling into braids
That overlay the rock,
Convey the bubbling fountains
Plumbed inside this gorge,
And bring to life
Attendant sprigs of emerald glow
Crocheted in crevices
That let the silver flow,
Extending privileges of green
To cool the canyon's crumpled
Slick rock serpentine.

An Inner Edge of Time

Far below the upper alcoves
And full-bellied bays,
Old grottoes tuck
Their beveled clefts of travertine,
And turquoise pools bend sunbeams down
To see the waving swords of light
Duel inside an underwater fight.

And we slip deeper into reverie
That skims some inner edge of time,
No more than spindrift figures
Fluttered past unfolded force,
Watching earthen actors one by one appear
To stride their monumental stage
And thunder through
The fable of creation here.

Idolatry of Chance

Recirculating waves crash back
Against the surge of forward breakers,
Fabricating hollow drops,
Extruding every kind of whiplash whirl
That flings such fever, foam, and spray
We could be on a roller coaster,
Clearly runaway
That hurtles past the gaping holes
And points of devil rock
That threaten from each place we glance,
As if to reaffirm some underlying
Wanton need for chance.

At Night on Sandbar Banks

And every night at dusk
We beach our rafts on sandbar banks
And ease into that interlude
Where episodes of day
Return as derring-do, as happy-ended play,
Until the urgency of night
Gallops in on thrashing legs
To launch afflicted sleep
Knotting into tangled dreams,
Each reoccurring scene
A charnel house, the place
Where people drowned convene.

Into Lava Falls

We rocket over entrance swells
And—wide-eyed—watch our raft
Miscarry, plunging straight into
The deepest, hardest-grinding hole
In all of Lava Falls.

Back-curling waves slam down,
Staving in the front, exactly where I sit
Holding two taut lines . . .
Now riding free, suspended in
A thick and greenish sea
That, no mistake,
Has gotten hold of me.

Stunned and spinning under,
Absent any sense of bearing,
Every action swimming in slow motion,
Final questions start to form:
Is this going to be . . .

But then the physics of inflation
And arcane configuration
Of displacement,
All the laws of energy
Converging
At the vortex of that hole,

Contrive to spit us out,
Return us to a sunlit world
Sweet and soft
With beating hearts and birds,
The sound of melody,
Each living tree

All seeming so unchastened
By our shock,
As we sit drenched
And gasping,
Stupid, grinning,
Free.

Jungles and Savannas

RAIN FORESTS, TROPICAL OR TEMPERATE, create for me a sense of lavish abundance, nature on the rampage, conditions meant for multiplication rather than the hard division of deserts. The poems here begin in the tepuis of southern Venezuela, ancient table mountains that were formed when Africa, India, Australia, and Antarctica were still joined in a huge protocontinent called Gondwana, the basis for Arthur Conan Doyle's novel *The Lost World*.

My first trip on the Amazon began at the mouth and went upriver a thousand miles to Manaus. This city was hacked out of jungle where the Rio Negro, itself the fifth largest river in the world, joins the Amazon. In the late 1800s rubber barons living there were so rich they built an opera house for the totally isolated city and brought Caruso to sing in it.

To get a better sense of the rain forest, two years later I flew over the spine of the Andes to the frontier town of Coca. Twelve of us went down the Rio Napo, one of two rivers that form the Amazon early in its thrust across the continent. Departing the longboat, we walked a path cleared by machete for about two miles before small dugout canoes took us across a lagoon. A lodge and bungalows connected by boardwalks rose out of rain and dank vegetation on the far side of the lagoon. That complete immersion into a crawling, humid world provided plenty of material for the four-part poem titled "Jungle Depths."

New Zealand's Milford Track was also high on my list of must-see places. This temperate rain forest gets nearly 400 inches of rain a year, a place of waterfalls and giant ferns, beech trees laden with moss, all rising out of mist, everything but the hobbits.

This thatched lodge and the bungalows attached by a boardwalk were home for a week in the Amazon jungle.

Daubing red paint on my face, and on the couple to my right, was a friendly act of welcome by the tribe we visited downriver.

The flat-topped tepuis are composed of twisted black rock, while pools of rainwater are tinted a copper color from the tannin in dead plant material and eroding crystals.

Next we shift to the great plains and savannas of Africa for poems that include several lion encounters and the opportunity to meet a young cheetah. Also, we'll observe the confidence and dignity of the people who predominate in this area, who seem to rule it, just as lions do within the animal kingdom—the Maasai.

The last two poems are set in Ethiopia. As part of a small adventure group, we traveled to the historical sites in the north, where Coptic Christians date back to biblical times, then moved on to the Muslim highlands in the east. The third leg of our travels, the most exciting for me, was in the south close to the borders of Kenya and Sudan. We drove down through the Great Rift Valley, past sunken lakes and white savannas, and spent time with tribal groups in the Omo River region. Though living fairly close to one another, the seven tribes we visited were surprisingly different—not only in appearance and the look of their villages, but in the sharply different attitudes with which they greeted us.

This young male cheetah was one of three brothers. His cool demeanor inspired the poem "Cheetah Rap."

The people of the Hamar Tribe were outgoing and friendly, and wore their traditional animal skins, bracelets, and necklaces. All of them—men, women, and children—had their hair arranged with a kind of red mud paste.

Venezuela's sheer-walled tepuis can rise as much as 5,000 feet from dense rain forest below.

The "Lost World"

Ancient Table Tops

Looming out of Mesozoic mist,
Bastions of a past
When continents were still conjoined
Persist mute and dumb, weathered numb,
Clad in prison gray, moldy bronze,
Splashed with cinnabar,
And leaking from a thousand places,
Water streaming down forsaken faces.

At their feet, heavy fragrance
Swirls through trees that wash the slopes,
While butterflies of startling iridescence
Ride the overheated breeze
And dodge reptilian tongues
As life divides and multiplies,
Rampant conjugation, naked saturation.

Across each fractured surface top
Gargoyles grumble, stone gone all awry,
Riddled into clefts and holes,
Become a home for pitcher plants
That open golden bowls
Enticing tiny animals to die.
Carnivorous bromeliads
And leaves of sundew lure
Hide the toads that swivel either eye,
Their wart or luminescent stripe
Warning of the poison pure.

Flowers wave adhesive nectar,
Fungi kill with yeast, nothing is released,
All are creatures caught
That cannot leave, cannot fly,
Trapped between the ticks of time
Atop these ancient tables in the sky.

A Hidden Pool

We groped into a narrow stream
Flowing from the semi-dark
Until it blossomed out, rounded into

Emerald eye that lay limpid,
Surface flecked in shards of sun,
A waterfall that fell five hundred feet
Spun into suspended spray
That moistened ferns, flowers, even trees
Set wet within the rocky face.

We frolicked, floated, gorged ourselves,
And dove beneath the shavings of its drop,
Then squatted down like crabs,
Arms and legs akimbo,
Wobbling over time-slick stone
On ledges overgrown in moss
That beaded from a thin veneer of dirt.

Gazing up where sky had opened clean
A fragile crack of blue, we felt detached
From everything we knew,
Spiraled into former time and space,
Spellbound in a place
So beautiful it hurt.

*A Pemón Indian led us up this stream that opened to
an astounding pool and waterfall.*

Jungle Depths

Rain

Furious clouds can take no more,
Sending rain in waves
That bruise already swollen sky,
Then swarm the forest canopy,
To ricochet off limbs and vines
And fall on broad banana leaves,
And gather, spent, in slumps of wet
Where creatures crouch, soaked, bent.

Scanty trails ooze
The mud that fastens onto every step,
That weeps excrescence of discarded life,
Sodden plant debris—yellow green—
Bits of organism spat between.

The storm moves on,
Leaves behind its heavy breath
Turned rank in tropic heat
Rising, steaming off the ground,
While gangling shafts of light
On pale stilts
Walk the jungle floor
Intent to randomly explore.

*This day was sunny. At other times the rain came down
so hard it seemed shot from guns.*

The Forest

Dislocated palms rear back
And straighten arching fronds
Beside the buttress roots of kapok trees.
Fuchsia clusters quiver.
Variegated orchids gleam
And long lianas loop and dangle
Twisted into snakes
As fungi fleck it all in flakes.

Morpho butterflies string blue
While other creatures creep and dart,
Swing in trees, or whine and lurk,
Proboscis poised, blood to boil,
Fever, death, their handiwork.

Bullet ants, an inch of vicious,
Bite whatever moves
Inflicting hours that radiate in pain,
Unlike leaf-cutter kin
That form a mile-long chain,
Each worker carting fresh-cut leaves
And overseen by beefy guards
That keep them on a plumb-straight line,
To feed their corpulence of queen
Who'll breed another horde,
Produced exactly in the ratios
Of this fixed, industrial design.

Everything adapts, tries to find a niche, and
somehow make a living.

Along the Waterways

Beside the wide lagoon
A coil of flattened grass
Suggests an anaconda there,
And four feet up a rosewood tree
The deep-clawed bark is telltale mark,
A jaguar prowling in the night,
Perhaps while we were on the water
Firing flashlight beams
At caiman eyes that flared a primal red
Until they'd dive beneath our sight.

Mangrove thickets mob the banks
And glisten in the morning sun
Where necklaces, superbly spun,
Are spread and on display,
Proprietors prepared to clutch and sting
And then begin to drain
The dead though still convulsing prey.

Strangler vines tie choking knots
On trees that struggle lifting up
Their racks of leaves, or falling short,
Contort to reach some sunshine spilled,
Where creatures camouflaged
Are seldom seen, and quickly gone,
And then it all repeats,
It all repeats.

*We learned there were ten things unseen for each one that
we noticed.*

High in the Canopy

Birds in chorus
Trill their melodies between
Each contrapuntal screech,
The notes all slicing down through
Layers of this forest world
To shape surreal music,
Soothe into an innocence
That covers up alarm,
Unwires the instincts meant for harm.

And sure enough a shrill-edged boom
Explodes in both my ears,
The sound of howler monkeys
Trooping through the forest top,
Cruising in that canopy of green,
Their moves a choreography
Conducted smooth and clean.

While down below my platform perch
Installed atop a kapok tree,
I chance to see the sudden flight
Of scarlet, gold, and blue macaw,
A brilliant colored thing
That garnishes the velvet light
Upon its synchrony of feathered wing,
Creating yet another proof
Of nature's deep nobility
And willingness to sing.

*I liked the rain forest best, to tell the truth, when a little bit
distanced from it, such as in this tree platform.*

Pure Primeval

We walk where ancient beeches brood,
Sodden trunks zippered up in moss,
Branches groaning in a muffled glow,
Weeping with the overflow,

A place where ferns unroll pubescent fronds
And waggle independent arms
Like giant spiders dipped in rust and green
Running riot through the scene,

Where sun looks in from time to time
And polishes the path, enlivens
Worn and flattened stone,
Refreshes lichen overgrown.

We enter gorges where the cliff sides spout,
Water hissing, cursing as it falls
On rocks, shatters into spray,
Quicksilver streams that run away,

Where bellbirds pipe their notes so crisp
They cleave the unity of time
Into diced intervals that fall
Between each reoccurring call.

Torrential rains and being continuously wet are often an integral part of this experience.

We tramp primeval track
Confronting glimpses of the past,
Our storehouse of realities reversed,
Piqued into a thirst

That goes unslaked, mortal beings raked
Too fast across abundance too profound
And then without a sound
And out of thick prehensile gloom

Huge incisors loom
Like relic teeth of shaved prehistory,
Destined here to be,
Burst free from deep within the Tasman Sea

That finishes our walk,
Negotiated with unruly space
That still remembers labored birth
And tries to keep command of earth.

The four-day walk ends where the land ends, at renowned Milford Sound.

The Solitary Maasai

He held the valley captive
With his confidence and grace,
Gliding through ancestral land
On sloping strides, an easy pace,
His bearing more than straight
And stronger yet than tall,
A sheer embodied fearlessness
Beneath that mountain wall.

We saw his red plaid robe,
Its declaration clear,
And saw the lengthy staff,
Or it might have been a spear,
And knew he was a warrior,
Killed a lion face to face,
For that Maasai rite of passage
Set the spirit of this place.

And when he reached the spot
Where we were watching, parked,
Apparently his journey's point
And we the target marked,
He stuck his head inside our car,
Spoke quickly to the guide
Asking with a wide-mouthed smile
If we'd please let him have a ride.

If one had to define the Maasai with a single word, "confidence" would be my first choice.

This cheetah never moved when we approached, totally cool, in control, man!

Cheetah Rap

been thinkin' that I'm feelin' really good
'bout aspects of the Cheetah brotherhood

got me an open, grassy view,
Mount Kenya tall and lookin' clear,
room to run if somethin' wrong appear

been eatin' full, no worries 'bout a meal,
jus' gonna chill, then do myself a stroll,
a li'l patrol . . . depend on how I feel

but when my pangs begin to bark and growl
get goin' on a badass prowl,
slip down into my flow, we call it stalk

hey baby, we ain't talkin' 'bout no walk,
you gonna see the way I hit each gear

turn on some crazy, turbonetic speed,
a blindin' bolt that do the deed

cuz I'm the fastest livin' thing on land,
ain't nothin' else come nowhere near,

and, dude, ya gotta check mah threads,
spot on appeal complete the real deal!

Etched

Eyes intense
Aimed unflinching stare
Into appraisal of
A meal there

Where we approached
The riverbank
Engrossed in crocodiles below,
So fascinated by
That grim reptilian sight,
Little did we know

Of instinct primed,
Destinies almost converged,
The lion well concealed,
Next appointment soon to be revealed

And then our late discovery,
Shouts and pell-mell flight,
Claws that meant to shred
Now etching memory
Instead.

Four of us, including the guide, were climbing out of our vehicle to see crocodiles in the river.
My wife, who stayed inside, first saw the lion barely 10 yards away.

This drama, played out in the dark, affected us more than the sight of kills during daylight hours.

Night Sounds on the Serengeti

Night followed dusk, followed day
And full of dinner, much to say,
We sat beside a fire warm and bright
Watching shadows dance
Within its orange, reassuring light.
Birds called out an evening song
And leaves swung softly in the dark.
Something moved beside a bush.
We heard a distant bark,

And then that shock wave blast
Of sudden thunder struck,
A huge reverberating roar
Blew away pretensions of that scene,
Followed quickly then by more
And, in between,
Receding screeches, something caught,
As if a violin's taut strings
Were ripping out.

When quiet came, it came extended
Like a tongue that probes
Incessantly at pain,
Swollen by the silence of the slain.

Mursi Woman

Mursi, Mursi, Mursi woman,
Lower lip enticingly enlarged,
Alluring plate slipped in,
That saucer of extension
Firm and round,

Focus of attention
When you were romanced,
Softest wedge of beauty
Pleasingly enhanced,
Suitors fetched, husband found,

Dowry calibrated to its size,
Wealth and status
Quite accordingly the prize,
Propriety and fashion both affirmed,
Beauty's fickle eye unbound.

Every aspect of this lady made a statement.

Ethiopian Gothic

Emerged from heat and dust
The image wrenched into resolve:

Two people worn away, bodies
Hung from faces
Nailed in place by eyes
That gnawed beneath the ribs and sag,
That haunted stillborn cries,
That warped the respite
Lodged in thatch and rag,

To blight each day,
Defeat the mind of hope
And even steal this moment
Meant for idle glance.

Expression sent
Across the blind divide of chance.

Her eyes spoke across the vast distance between us,
and beyond.

Earth and Human Spirit

The Jain temple at Ranakpor in Rajasthan, India, was begun in 1440 and took fifty years to complete.

This old watchtower broods over the Cliffs of Moher on the west coast of Ireland.

MANY OF MY POEMS infuse a human perspective into descriptions of earth's "eloquent" landforms. The poems grouped here reverse the focus, looking at the people and their complex interaction with the land. The first poem observes Jain priests in India who go from birth to death with only three possessions—a begging bowl, a whisk to sweep their path, and a thin mat on which to sleep. They wear no clothing, as we noticed while passing several walking toward a temple. I didn't intrude on their smiling, good nature to take a picture. The photo beside my poem is of a statue inside the temple.

The beautiful, sometimes melancholy southwestern coast of Ireland is where earth's largest landmass, Eurasia, reaches its westernmost point and crashes into the sea. That sense of geographic finality, as well as centuries of being underdog to the British, not to mention Viking raids earlier on, endures within the people. But their sorrow and world-weariness have been softened by a charm and grace that lift the spirit, unless it breaks your heart first. It is Irish after all.

Before reaching Tierra del Fuego, the end of inhabited land on earth, we stop beneath the Andes in Argentina, where large estancias range across tawny colored pampas, often next to elongated silver lakes holding remains of glaciers. One glacier, Perito Moreno, is still advancing and for me conjured feelings of soldiers being pushed to a battlefront.

On the Yangtze River in 1998, going through its famous gorges, we felt the majesty of that river. An exhibit at the huge dam, under construction then, showed how far waters would rise in the future. My poem reflects on the issue: humans by the billions with real needs are emerging toward better lives after millennia of fragile, often heartbreaking existence. Yet development comes with a cost—how much of the wild, raw essence of the earth must we lose? Encroachments at the nearly ethereal mountain shapes near Guilin, also in China, pose the same question.

Sky Clad People

Naked
Hairless
    plucked smooth
Smiling
    on this road

Possessing just:
    a bowl
        for water and
        each gift of food
    a whisk
        to sweep the path
        and take no life
    a mat
        to place upon the ground
        and rest at night
    the wet of monsoon rains
    the warmth of sun
    all scents
    the stars

To be:
    from birth
        until they die
    Jain priests
        clad only by the sky.

Only the highest, most exalted class of Jain priests still practices this
extreme asceticism.

This poem nods in remembrance of Dylan Thomas and his
"Do Not Go Gentle into That Good Night."

The Irish Coast

Dingle Peninsula

Flanks green and gleaming
Breathing hard with hope, enamored
Of the curving sun,
Softness of the sod,
Hearts yearning west to stay with day,
Are stunned.

Screaming at the wind, heavy fisted,
Hurling rocks against the tide,
Against the waning light,
Against the craven subterfuge of night,
They turn a shoulder to the sea
And stand alone,
Tears dried, strewn in stone,
Aching westward, want denied,
Ending here to be.

Skellig Islands

Ghost ships anchored
To the simple sea
Leak of Druids,
Monks dispatched,
Marauding Vikings unredeemed,

Where blood that dripped
Through fallen walls
Withstands the purity of sky.
And ocean swells
Do not wash clean.
Forever stained.

Islands anchored there
Among the things unseen.

*Viking raids in the ninth century took a heavy toll on the quiet
Christian monasteries located on these islands.*

Connemara

Rhododendron climbs on lilt and lattice
Stretching blossoms high,
Ignored by condescending sky
Self-absorbed above the ground.

Emboldened lakes stare steely blue
With cold that nips the land, but nourishes
The reeds that bend at every wind command
And make their nodding little simpered sound.

Mountains now gone deaf, look barren, old,
Yet huff above deep-layered land below,
Where peat bogs talk flambeau, yet grovel
Unresolved in troubled ground,

Until they get themselves dug out
And set on fire, to crackle and inspire
The Irish glow that brightens every wound,
Make sure there's hurt enough to go around.

At a bar in Galway two happy patrons said I looked like someone from Connemara. Actually, my Irish ancestors came from County Cork.

The climate is somewhat better than its reputation, especially considering that the place is only 700 hundred miles from Antarctica.

Tierra del Fuego

Lashed by wind
And whipped by wild seas,
Fearful sailors in their quest
To round the Horn
Saw blazes warming huddled habitants
And called this place the land of fire—
Confusion overwrought with scorn.

That appellation lingers on,
An irony affixed to such a place
Of frozen gales
That force each bush and tree to bend,
To cling in sore resistance
'Til the sea in mercy rises up
And thunders unequivocally
That all the land shall end.

A distant and forsaken isle
Beyond the cold Magellan strait,
It shivers under overbearing clouds
And stakes a fragile sense of worth
Upon the proud, eccentric claim
To be that final piece of land
Inhabited on earth.

This glacier in Patagonia is one of the few in the world that is advancing.

An Advancing Glacier

Like an army massed
And marching to a cause unknown
This glacier moves,
Its ranks grinding forward,
Pressing closer to the front
Until in time each one becomes
The foremost wall,

Standing frozen, shocked,
And forced to teeter, twist,
Then take the booming crack
That sounds like cannon fire,
And fracture blue as lapis lazuli
And drop into finality.

Shattered fragments float,
Their broken faces pale, appealing
To the sun
Which soon betrays them with its heat—
Never knowing why
Their glacier happened to advance
When others just retreat.

The Southern Cross

Flung down beneath some trees
While temperatures still soared,
Our camp began to feel confined,
The conversation bored
And so we left the place
To walk in moonless night
Within a region far removed
From any civilizing light.

We climbed an arching rock,
Leaned back on curls of heat
And gazing higher, eyed infinity,
The Milky Way a rhythm of repeat,
An incantation trying to reel us in,
A vast and intricate ballet,
Its stars all dancing full of chatter,
Sharing cosmic interplay.

And lying on our backs, absorbed
Into the palace of that sky,
I swear those stars began to beckon,
Coaxing us to fly,
To leave this rock, this weary earth
And feel no sense of loss,
Just reach into the heavens now
And grasp the Southern Cross.

*This is the sky we saw in Australia's Outback that night. The Southern Cross, so important to mariners
in olden days, is located center-right, beside the black, kite-shaped space.*

Yangtze Gorges

I

Reckless dragon snorts, claws,
Mountains sundered bleed into the slash.
The river thunders,
And the peaks astride this beast
Look down ill at ease,
Knob and tremble in their knees.

Ancient earth gates open,
Gorges writhe in rhythm
Meant to squeeze and steer
The nearly strangled river
Through its labored passage here.

Wild persimmon trees
And green, luxuriant bamboo
Hurry up the slopes,
Yet human schemes pursue.

II

Yes, the waters rose, stalked
Those terraces and walls, flowers, trees
That drank sweet drafts of sky,
Where villages held thin-boned homes,
Tried to keep them dry,

But felt the rising tongue slip in,
Drag them to the swirl, down into the dread,
Silhouettes of towns submerged,
Silt and sadness, all the quiet dead.

*As a result of the great dam, there is a new source of electricity and periodic floods are averted, but also
more than a million people have been displaced and a natural treasure altered—forever.*

Beside the River Li

Silken mist and polished
Particles of jade
Catch on upturned teeth,
And try to cushion every bite
So not to lacerate the sky.

Softened, long reclusive forms
Grope like gnarled hands,
The twisted fingers of old beings
Reaching from another world
To speak in signs,
To stroke their age-old meaning
Into mystic shapes
That flow beside the River Li.

Poets, artists, dreamers trace
Each curve and angle
On the fabric of their minds,
But find that nothing fits,
Even time retreats,
Becomes a distant music
Floating past disheveled domes,
Mingled with the mist and jade
Content into eternity.

The strange, verdant shapes seem to speak directly to the soul.

Four colossal statues of Ramses ll at Abu Simbel, Egypt.

Among the Ruins of Antiquity

"Moderation is a fatal thing. Nothing succeeds like excess."
—Oscar Wilde

Testimony

THERE IS MAGIC IN RUINS. They whisper to us of the past, telling stories of grand schemes and the nobility, or tragedy, of human aspiration. Caught in the grip of nature, there is often an urgency to the voice. And where we begin, at Chaco Canyon in northern New Mexico, there is also a continuing mystery. The Pueblo culture there flourished until the late thirteenth century, when everyone suddenly departed.

Then we skip to Myanmar in southeast Asia to visit Bagan where thousands of temples were abandoned at about the same time, 1297 to be exact. But that is no mystery. They were fleeing armies of Kublai Khan, who chose not to destroy the place. In the year 1310, Muslim invaders left the city of Khajuraho in India, but also decided to leave its temples with their richly erotic, unabashedly explicit, sexual scenes largely intact.

Next, we'll visit lands with fabled sites close to the Mediterranean Sea, first contemplating Palmyra during its Roman rule, then considering the story of St. Simeon, also in Syria, who lived thirty years at the top of a pillar preaching total self-denial. We'll enter the striking ruins at Petra in Jordan, called "the rose-red city half as old as time" in a sonnet by John Burgon in 1845. After the churches of Lalibela in Ethiopia, also hewn out of rock, two poems are set in Egypt. One considers the transformative gifts of the Nile River. The other celebrates pleasures to be found in ruins at Luxor.

The coliseum at Pula on the Dalmatian coast in Croatia was built in the reign of Augustus and is one of the six largest surviving Roman amphitheaters in the world. Spectacles, usually with gladiators, continued there until the fifth century.

Poems set in Greece and Italy range from the sublime beauty of the Parthenon to the lonely ruins of a Greek temple in Sicily. In Pompeii, I try to imagine that fateful day in the year A.D. 79 when "earth died." Then we'll move on to the Silk Road in China, Pakistan, and Uzbekistan, which has a separate introductory section.

The Anasazi's sudden departure continues to perplex archaeologists and anthropologists.

Chaco Canyon

Creases of preconscious presence
Riddled with encoded essence
Cast an earthbound spell
That haunts the ruins here,
Sliding fingers over walls,
Stirring dust in kivas,
Forming phantom shapes
That mount the desert wind
To ride across unconquered night
And mourn extinct domain.

Convincing stones remain
That astronomically align,
That spell intrigue beyond design,
A teeming complex cast aside,
Reasons unrevealed—
Buried with burnt ends of bitter bone,
And layers yet unknown,
The grist for steady efforts to explain.

Of thirteen thousand temples built in the tenth and eleventh centuries, some two thousand still remain.

Kingdom of Bagan

South of Mandalay
Within an Irrawaddy bend,
Two thousand temples rise and blink
In orotund display,
Extend their gift another day.

They glory in the burnished gold
And pure celestial white,
Or subtlety of sun burnt brick,
All thrusting up from storied ground
To sculpt this kingdom crowned,

Where life was suddenly withdrawn,
Where kings and people fled,
Abandoned every treasure of Bagan
To flee from marching armies
Of the cold-faced Kublai Khan,

Leaving here in quiet residence
Upon this never-equaled plain,
The temples of that early reign
To work their holy wonder once again.

Temples of Khajuraho

Odes to ecstasy,
Professions of fertility,
Temples made to climb,
To throb and soar
In sure vitality,
Their undulating lines
Free of limits,
Free of stone confines.

Facades alive and gleaming
Rise in high relief,
Principles of universe
Carved in aspiration
Resonate with
Rich erotic decoration.
Every curve, contortion
Perfect in proportion

Balanced into bliss
Beyond caress or kiss.
Men engulfed, wives inclined,
Lovers intertwined,
No hint of base profanity
Within this joyous,
Fruitful, dear
Humanity.

Some say every position in the Kama Sutra
is represented somewhere on these temples.

Palmyra

It was a crossing point of caravans,
An old oasis filled with palms
That sipped from deep beneath the sand,
Until it sprang into a princely place,
An outpost of imperial command.

Its chorus rang with shouts and shops,
Cobbled streets and lofty colonnades,
An arched praetorian gate,
As well as legions sent to occupy
The strong-willed, partly Persian state.

Good citizens indulged their theater,
Grand temples gleamed, and baths
Were shaped with marble balustrade,
But only statues on their pedestals
Dared mix with soldiers on parade.

The city gloried in its grandeur, rolled
In riches tied to trading routes
Strategically imposed by Rome,
But left those men sent tramping there
A thousand lonely leagues from home.

The finished sun now slips away
Leaving just its rose and dusty glow
To tint these broken temple walls,
Pillars, pediments still on display,
Old ruins rouged for this, their final show.

Day ends in a blaze of sun, and you can almost hear Roman soldiers tramping through the arched praetorian gate.

St. Simeon's Pillar

His fame had claimed the century.
Roads were choked with those
Arrived to see this man
Exhorting all to self deny,
Let go each earthly thing,
Reject all comfort, even space.

That's how he lived for thirty years,
Roosted fifty feet into the sky,
Enduring there malnourished and exposed,
Eating scarcely once a week,
Yet preaching rabid abstinence
Until the shriveled day he died.

The largest church in all of Christendom
Was built with an enormous dome
To house the pillar that he'd occupied,
And for another seven hundred years
Pilgrims traveled there to see his perch,

And often let their hands
Remove a tiny piece of stone
As relic of his strong, astringent grace,
Leaving now but three-foot nub,
And no haranging from that fervent face.

St. Simeon died in the year 459 near Aleppo, Syria, after living for more than
thirty years atop a pillar.

Petra

Pillars prop a past expired long ago,
A city hidden deep in folds of rock,
Its people living rich,
Exploiting drama and mystique,

Who turned the only entrance into shock—
Approached by winding through a narrow cleft,
A rocky corridor they called the "siq"—
Which opens to reveal

In monumental elegance,
Both stunning and sublime…
Their "rose-red city half as old as time."

Two millennia ago, clever Nabateans prospered by extracting
payment for their "protection" of each caravan passing by.

Rock-Hewn Churches
of Lalibela

Incised four stories deep,
Churches hewn eight hundred years ago
Abide in beds of rock
And hide their weathered piety
Below the surface planes of sight.

Hermits sit in shallow caves
That pock the inner space
Peeling layers off intensive faith
Like onion skins pulled loose,
Examined in the filtered light,
Until each flutters down
To fluff a bed for rag and bone,
The selfsame graves that follow life
In consecration of a holy place.

*Churches were carved below ground in the Christian
north of Ethiopia.*

Dreams along the Nile

The sun in burning silence
Saw you take possession of this land,
Gliding over desert sand
To designate the future way,
And leave a residue of dreams
That endlessly replay:

    you wash papyrus banks
    and tease the lotus so alluring
    down beside the yielding palms

    you summon birds and serpents,
    lions, crocodiles

    you flow your vital stream
    that brings to life the green

    that fashions new societies,
    conjoins the lands

    and in triumphant mood
    you raise pharaohs high,
    their shadows long

Allowing dreams to grow,
Forever know your cradle song.

The Nile, which gave rise to the Egyptian civilization, often overflows its banks.

The Ruins at Luxor

Do not be fooled by surfaces
Now full of fracture and decline.
Luxor lives
And dwells along the Nile
Disdainful of the desert's creep,
Sufficient stones in place
To easily rebut the sand
And strut in its heroic space.

Stripped and ravaged long ago,
Cast off by thieves and left to die
Beneath the scarifying sky,
Its heat and anger fused
Into a passion bared
For pleasure down in dust,
Ruination and decay
Redressed in disarray.

No former glory gone—
This current life appended to the past—
Luxor stands astride the sweep of time
Transfigured from its prime,
But pulsing, proud, alive,
The redolence in ruin sweet beyond
Mere satisfaction to survive.

*Magnificent structures live on at Luxor, once
the ancient city of Thebes, powerful capital of
Upper Egypt.*

Gladiators battled to the death for twenty-three thousand spectators in this coliseum.

The Maximus of Must

Enter this arena, gladiator,
Face the quickly hurled spear,
The whippet bite of blade,
Hammer spiked and chained to crushing ball
And, gladiator, think about the crowd,
Fate is more than foe for those who fall—
Life will balance on the dazzle of your show.

Make them shriek, gladiator,
Work that crass, conflicted crowd,
Engage impulses twitching at each loin,
Elicit rounds of empathetic gasp,
Feed each patron's subtleties of need,
For every thumb's a scale, gladiator,
Calibrated to your thrust,
Your maximus of must:
Slay, or you'll be slain,
But fight the fight, that fallen, win!

Feel the rolling wave, gladiator,
Gauge collective lust,
Lift their eyes into a warm reprieve
That trumps the twisted grin,

Twenty thousand gods weighing in.

Pompeii

Incandescent forces build beneath
The rumbling mountain stare
Where molten tongues
Probe a long-tumescent tear
Waiting for their god to nod:

    Vulcan's fire flung,
    Vesuvius to roar,
    Earth to die

Beneath the sky that fell one day
And so immortalized Pompeii.

Ash and sulfur settle
Over pockets of escaping screams
Where fresh digested rock
Flooding downward over slopes,
Stiffens shock
Into the rictus of abandoned hopes.

Pursuit of life and bread and pleasure
Snuffed in midday night,
Forever fossilized as testament
Unto that Armageddon might

Beneath the sky that fell one day
And so immortalized Pompeii.

*These plaster casts re-created body spaces of victims—exactly as they were found—
during excavations in 1860.*

Pale Temple

You came in grace and Greek intent
To live as close companion to the sea,
Take in its tonic draft of salt-singed air,
Extol the friendly shores of Sicily.

Untoppled columns stand erect
Still lending form and beauty here,
Exemplars meant to calm this coast
Where fields slope down and disappear.

The sun in warm abundance beams
Caressing broken temple brows,
But cannot ease your loneliness
That whispers out to pine and olive boughs.

The ruins of this Greek temple on the southern shore of Sicily date back to the fifth century B.C.

Athenians planned the Parthenon right after their victory at Marathon, but it had to wait forty years—until Pericles became king—before coming to fruition.

To Find the Parthenon

I want to stand with Pericles
And find my way into his triumph,
Logic curved into such beauty
Fluid, fresh, incumbent in
The form and space,

Before that litany of follies
Fell upon the place,
Before skullduggery
By Persians, Franks, and Catalans,
Venetians, then Teutonic hordes,
The constant warring Turks,

Before those practice rounds
Were fired,
Before the British quietly arranged
To carry off its works,
Before the quakes and smog
And other jealousies conspired.

Could I please see the way it was
In those precocious days
Of bloom and undefiled grace
When Greece was Greece
And glory knew
To smile upon a perfect face?

The Silk Road

"I did not tell half of what I saw, for no one would have believed me."

— Marco Polo (on his deathbed)

T HE SILK ROAD may have been the most important trade route in history. From the second century B.C. until after Marco Polo's journey in the late thirteenth century, caravans carried precious cargoes across China and central Asia, linking East and West and, in the process, transporting cultures, peoples, and religion.

The seven poems here follow my travels west across China and on to Samarkand, now in Uzbekistan. They provide glimpses along this fabled route, beginning with the famous "terra-cotta army" in Xi'an, the old capital of China. More than eight thousand life-size figures wear battle attire and facial expressions modeled on soldiers of the emperor's army.

At the oasis of Dunhuang, we'll visit the Mogao caves, carved over a period of twelve hundred years and filled with statues of the Buddha and brilliant murals, which form the greatest trove of Buddhist art in the world. After speculating on the mindset of a 70-foot Buddha etched into limestone beside the Yellow River, we look in on the dead city of Jiaohe. It is a particularly haunting place, where all human life ended at the hands of Genghis Khan and his invading Mongols.

We proceed to the place where China ends at Kashgar, where five major mountain ranges hem three sides and the Taklimakan, considered the world's most inhospitable desert, lies in the fourth. Kashgar is the place where British India, Russia, and China jousted for nearly a hundred years (from 1813 to 1907) to gain control of central Asia. Through all of that, it remains true to its Muslim roots. The huge and lively Sunday Market there is an exotic, unforgettable experience.

Once over the mountain knot, we journey into Pakistan and the magical kingdom of Hunza, renowned for scenery and the longevity of its people. We end at Samarkand, the storied crossroads of nearly all Silk Road travel and the capital city of an empire founded by Tamarlane.

This army of terra-cotta soldiers was created to protect Qin Shi Huang, first emperor of all China (211–206 B.C.).

The Emperor's Last Campaign

The Emperor Qin went quietly to war,
His army drilled, embedded, well prepared
To fight an unknown enemy
Whose destiny perchance he shared.

Soldiers bristled, columns set inside
A cunning, predetermined place,
Each man reflecting on old battles fought,
Expression fixed upon his face.

That force—eight thousand strong—deployed
Beneath the ground was willing then
With sword and spear and scimitar
To face whatever foe, those terra-cotta men

Who've waited here through two millennia,
Standing vigilant and brave,
Their mission to protect the Emperor Qin
Resting in his monumental grave.

The Ming Sha Dunes, highest in the Gobi Desert, arch into the sky at Dunhuang.

Dunhuang

Intrepid caravans pushed west,
Lurching with their burden
Spun from Eastern mystery,
The goods more valuable than gold,
Produced to cling and dazzle and caress
Rich and noble Roman ladies,
Drape their senators in opulence,
And dress the Greeks and Byzantines
In silken soft compliant fold.

And in return
Impressive cargoes traveled to Cathay
With sandalwood and jade,
Casks of frankincense and myrrh.
Music of the West went East,
Lute and oboe, and the flute,
Followed by the Buddha,
Wonders of his wisdom
Came of age along this route.

But transport of such treasure
Called for journeys past extreme
Facing mountains, canyons, brigands,
Floors of desert desolation
Poised to snatch all life,
Returning only ghosts
To twitch and keen at each remote mirage,
Remnant of the confrontation.

Scheming masters of that trade,
Those richly robed grandees,
Sought caravans of lucky destiny
And tried to buy the Buddha's help
With art and sculpture, lavish adulation
Offered here in age-old sophistry.

And so, Dunhuang,
This old oasis crossroads,
Distant point of no return
Where giant dunes arch into the sky
Like beacon signals shining clear,
Became the spot where merchants
Weighed the treasure of their dreams
Against the dagger of their fear

And carved five hundred caves,
Buddha seated, hand upraised
To soothe the latencies of fate,
Each wall adorned in intricate tableaux,
Twelve hundred years
Of hope and passion still aglow,
And filled with timeless grace
Inside the desert's dry, indifferent face.

Frescoes and sculpture are different from cave to cave, reflecting changes in prevailing artistic styles over the centuries of continued creation.

Buddha by the River

Giant Buddha—
Carved from ancient cliff side
In the time of T'ang,
You sit in silence
By that river, Yellow River,
Watching millions swirl
Through lives of turbulence and sorrow.

Great colossal Buddha—
Talismanic tall,
Your lips turn down, eyes squeeze tight,
No hint of hope
Not even of compassion!
Must you dwell detached
As if uncaring, cold,
Beholden to some inner truth
That mortals cannot share,
Cannot even borrow?

Or is your face a mask
That hides much deeper love,
Created stern to parry all requests
For comfort and illusion,
Meant to nudge these mortals forward
Fathoming for light
To find and shape their own tomorrow!

*This Buddha, rising more than 100 feet beside
the Yellow River, is in the geographic center of
present-day China.*

Jiaohe was established in the first century B.C. and existed for fifteen hundred years until a Mongol invasion led by Genghis Khan brought it to an end.

Jiaohe Was Its Name

No scent of spices on the breeze,
Nor men with ripened melons
In deep-shaded corners of the square.
Silence now where laughter rang
From sprawling caravansaries,
Where brazen days of desert hardship
Loosened over skewered meat
And climbing curlicues of smoke.

And only whispered sounds of sand
Sliding ever in upon itself,
Replacing sighs gone out
From maidens dancing over dunes
To meet their lovers
In deep creases of approaching night.

Yet still—through squinted eyes—
At the piercing moment of each dawn
A trailing echo can be heard,
The Mongols' terrifying cry
Resounding from the thirteenth century
When they rode hard,
The north wind at their backs,
And overran this slender place.

And since that day, the wind alone
Seeks out these corridors,
And only dust of memories
And desiccated fragments of old anguish
Linger on in cracks of mud-brick walls.

Jiaohe was its name.

More than fifty thousand people converge each week at the Kashgar Sunday Market.

Kashgar and Its Sunday Market

Overgrown oasis, scrap of Turkestan,
Beckons from behind its curtain of intrigue,
Where spies from British India
Had jousted Russians sneaking south,
And Chinese came to stay,
But left two thousand years of roots in place
That grow toward Mecca every day.

Prodigious mountains hem three sides
And on the fourth a hellish desert reigns
Where sands first freeze before they burn,
Where storms blacken daytime sky
And those who enter mostly die.

Yet, traveler come, behold . . .
Be dazzled by this city living legend,
Feel its ages past,
The stain of old conspiracies,
Treasures torn from musty cupboards,
Reek and sweepings off the floor,
The center of a continent erupted

Into market pandemonium
That revels in uproar.

Carts of fresh cut timber,
Goats trotting in to market,
Blacksmiths at their forge
Beside the pots and rusty tools,
Porcelain and jewels;
Tattooed hands of Uighur women
Sifting bolts of cloth
Where tunic, pantaloon, and suit
Are strung on string
And billowing.

Pyramids of fruit, spices piled
To form an aromatic mound,
Pepper being ground,
Braziers overlaid with meat
And breads baking, stacked, round,
Next to strange elixirs, tea,
Water-sellers roaming free.

Falcons on their trainers' wrists,
Pigeons lifted out of baskets,
Camels bartered, bought
Beside the racks of fur and hide,
Not far from steely knives
Enclosed within a decorated sheath,
While Kazakhs gallop horses,
Stopping now and then
To show the flanks and teeth.

Turkish barbers shaving faces,
Heads as bald as melons,
Trimming wispy beards
Of patriarchs,
While patients sit on carpets
Spread with pills and potions,
Bottles luminescent,
Greenish oil next to toad
And dried snake in harmless coil.

Menders cutting, stitching,
Doing quick repairs,
Purveyors pacing, fingers
Floating over wares,
Ladies robed head to toe,
Each bobbing moon of veiled face
Deflecting heathen glances,
Other costumes sheer
Beneath the smiles
Meant to be appealing.

Men in skullcap, breeches,
Heavy boot and sash
And crescent eyes that flash
Collective memories of
The Golden Horde and Genghis Khan,
Tajik tribesmen down
From pastures of the high Pamirs,
Squinting in the light,
Faces furrowed, bone tight,
Blackened by the sun,

The same sun that sinks now
Stretching shadows low,
Painting purple fusion
Onto coming dusky night,
Where raucous waves of market din
That only hours ago
Resounded like a heavy sea,
Soften into zephyrs
Soothing every family.

Children sleep,
Mothers soon to snuggle in
With fruit and squash and water pot,
Fathers reining donkeys
Over broken roads
Leading back to mud brick homes
Flung out across this worn oasis
Where the hinterland extends,
Disappearing into quiet spaces
Of this ancient place where China ends.

Hunza

Land of legend, Shangri-la
That fell between a time and place
On terraces of startled space
Ensnaring traders, pilgrims, soldiers,
Roaming Turks and Persians,
Mongols from the Khan descended,
Blue-eyed Macedons whose Alexander
Came this way,

All who chose to stay,
Who fashioned fort and castle into Kingdom,
Channeled snow to flow,
To seep and murmur
Under flower-fragrant orchards,
People living lives
Unbridled and extreme,
Twisted into tensile strength,
Longevity renowned and rare,

Ripened from an odd ambrosia:
Apricots and wheat
And savage mountain splendor
Clarified in crystal empty air.

*Hunza is a timeless place, the model for Shangri-la in
James Hilton's novel* Lost Horizon.

Samarkand

Facades supreme, pretentious, bold,
Laced with gold, confess
Their domes of raw indulgence,
Minarets and great madrassas,
Flowers fed from ravaged land:
The marveled sight of Samarkand.

Plunder, riches, pillage,
Populations murdered
Paled into a bloodless blue
Before they cringed green
And rose above the scene,
Born again as turquoise tiles.

Artisans alone reprieved, brought here
To spin the spoils into treasure,
Arabesques radiating pleasure
Opulent as Tamerlane was cruel,
Hard coin of his malignant rule.

*In the late 1300s Tamerlane laid waste to most of the
capitals of central and southern Asia, gaining the riches
to give this city its splendor.*

Chacabo Indians in a dugout canoe paddle across an inundated forest in Amazonia.

Raw Adventures

"There is nothing hidden by the earth, but time shall bring it forth into the sunlight."
—Horace

Ali and Alberto stand beside piled stones marking the route north to the Taoudenni mine.

Dots are numbered to follow the poem sequence but are positioned on the map exactly where the picture was taken.

Whenever possible, we camped beside sand dunes, both for shelter and for the appealing sight.

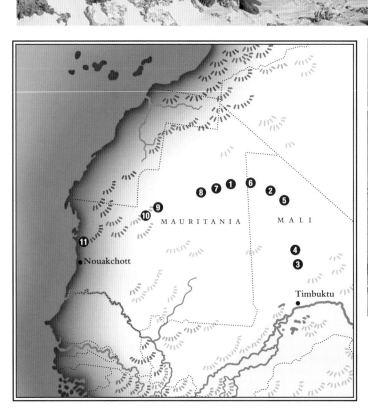

MAURITANIA   MALI

Nouakchott

Timbuktu

The Ultimate Sahara Expedition

AN ADVENTURE COMPANY'S 2001 catalog caught my eye with a trip never offered before, called the Ultimate Sahara Expedition. It was to begin in Timbuktu and go north to the infamous Taoudenni salt mine, then turn west and cross the emptiest, least known portion of the Sahara. The leader would be Alberto Nicheli, who had a reputation as an Indiana Jones character. The trip description made it clear there was no guarantee of success; only persons willing "to roll with the punches" should apply.

Six of us signed up. Our caravan consisted of three Toyota Land Cruisers and two trucks loaded with supplies. The Tuareg staff included a cook, his assistant, a mechanic, four drivers, and, to our surprise, two tough looking armed guards carrying rifles and Kalashnikovs. Also, and perhaps most important to success of the endeavor, we had Ali.

Alberto knew the desert, was resourceful, and had maps, a GPS, and an indomitable spirit. But Ali was a man *of* the desert. He had ridden caravans as a child and had guided countless expeditions. Alberto would pinpoint our route on his maps, then Ali would read the desert—feel the sand, study the shapes of dunes, sight the lines of escarpment walls and tell us how to get through. Not that we didn't get stuck, on average three or four times a day. We'd exit the vehicle, the driver would dig out the wheels, place aluminum tracks underneath, and accelerate just enough—while we pushed—to creep out of the hole instead of spinning in deeper.

For three days we traveled north to the Taoudenni mine, which was worked by slaves for nearly two thousand years, then became a notorious prison. Along the way ten camel caravans passed us in a steady, mesmerizing rhythm, and we encountered one small village and several wells with camels, goats, donkeys, and friendly Tuaregs.

Our driver, Hadji, had been a bandit, smuggler, and soldier in the Tuareg Rebellion, and he still drove as if he were escaping from something.

A caravan-style tented "hotel" was offered, but we wanted to continue camping on our last two nights in the desert. From left: Carol, Alberto, Jaime, and myself.

After looking at the mine, we headed west into a vertiginous expanse of remote, almost empty desert. Two days later, after we had encountered a smuggler's truck hauling French cigarettes and crossed the border between Mali and Mauritania, Alberto explained the reason for our armed guards. He had tried this trip four months earlier with a French group. Camped outside the Taoudenni mine, at the same spot where we had spent the night, he was awakened at dawn by truck engines and the rat-a-tat-tat of Kalashnikov fire. Bandits forced everyone out of their tents and into the spread-eagle position on the sand, then took all money and valuables, most of the expedition supplies, and two Toyotas. Following the code of the desert, they left the group with just enough to get back to Timbuktu. So for our trip, his second try, Alberto came prepared.

For the next ten days, we saw very little that was alive. The weather changed from hot to cold and back to hot. We endured two sandstorms. The terrain shifted from dunes to vast flat basins and rocky escarpments. We saw petroglyphs of cattle, trees, and hippopotami etched five thousand years ago, when the desert was green and flowing with water. After a drive through the brutal Richat Crater, the gearbox of one of our Toyotas broke and the vehicle had to be abandoned. (Alberto would retrieve it later, on his return trip with a different group.)

Each day and night brought adventure, obstacles, and delights. In late afternoon, we'd find the best available campsite, often nestled into sand dunes. After the staff unloaded gear and set up for dinner and all of us had arranged our tents for the night, Alberto would bring out good wine, Scotch, and vodka and we'd have a surprisingly well-cooked dinner. He'd put on a music tape and turn up the volume, one night Rachmaninoff, the next the Buena Vista Social Club, and under the stars a thousand miles from nowhere we felt halfway to infinity.

We Came to Find Adventure

The notion grew from deep inside a dream,
Retrace the route of ancient caravans,
Intent to roll completely through
An empty, near vertiginous expanse,
The artistry of inching
Pushed two thousand miles
Across the sand's far-fetched audacity,

Accordingly,
We took the dunes as they arrived
And jostled over stone with grins,
And laughed when we got stuck
Or while we masticated grit,
Then had two cups of water for a wash
Before the time to sleep
In creases of beguiling dunes,
Or lacking sand, atop a pebble field,
Or in some gap
Within a running spell of rocks.

It really mattered not . . .
We'd come to pick the whole Sahara crop,
We'd come to find adventure, friend,
And that is what we got.

Our desert-savvy guide, Alberto Nicheli, had dreamed of
crossing this little known portion of the Sahara for more
than twenty years.

Centered on Survival

Harshest driest essence tamped
into a crucible of earth

Elements all pared,
stripped and irreducible,

Each living thing
centered on survival.

Requisites for being, everything
we'd ever known, were gone

And what was left, what remained,
emptied to a void

Vast and whole, hardened inward,
turned completely cruel

Connecting us—so odd it seemed—
to deeper meaning

And renewal.

*This camel was the only living thing we saw
for miles.*

Ten caravans passed in eerie silence on our way to the Taoudenni mine.

Camel Caravans

Dimly distant they appear
Assembled out of heat and haze,
Emerging proud, erect, aloof,
A single file of linked nobility,
Each camel mantled,
Burdened with four blocks of salt
And seldom brought to halt.

In silence passing by
They verge into a vision
Fading soon to far horizon line,
Their strides released in angled arcs
That meet and cup the sand,
And set a motion flowing,
Near sublime,
That strokes its earnest rhythm
Down into the earth,
To take a place
With all the caravans of time.

Araouane

Hard distance north of Timbuktu
A village lies half buried,
Flotsam snagged,
Inhabitants exposed and wriggling
On their barren land.

The fort alone looks rooted, strong,
Resisting waves of desert
Heaved against its brace, but often
Wind swoops in to seize the sand
And fills great howling clouds,
Then wrings them down upon the place.

People shrink and parry,
Hunker down inside their dread
And dream about escape,
But live on margin streaked with fear
And plead for truce instead,
Though in a servile voice
The desert does not hear.

This was the first—and only—village we saw until four days before our journey ended.

The mine operates now with contract labor, but only for the cooler half of the year from October to March.

Salt Mines at Taoudenni

Appalling heat secures a heavy lid
Upon this cauldron filled with bone,
The residue reminder
Of its centuries with slaves.

Adding to those early graves,
It was a prison for some fifty years,
Stalking thieves and nightmare
Of unfavored politician's fears,
Where Westerners were put to death
If caught while passing by,
And convicts working in their rows
Were meant to desiccate and die.

But now the men arrive with hope,
And chisel out, then scrape and shape
The caustic blocks of salt,
Feeling grateful for their pay,
A pittance more than cost of bread,
The chance to take some money home
Unless they leave Taoudenni dead.

Borders

Borders sneak and creep,
Devise a way to infiltrate
And separate the land.
They trace convexities of dunes,
Inscribe each angle claimed by rock
And outline paths
Of rivers now run dry.

Further, so it seems,
They'll reenact abstractions
Inked on maps and charts,
Defining where one country ends,
Another starts,
Reflecting sovereign rights to rule,
Religions clashed,
Devoted armies to command.

And when we reach our crossing point,
Islamic Mauritania ahead
And multicultured Mali left behind,
An odd platoon appears—
Each figure squatting low, dug in,
As if to guard their proud, unsullied land
Against the heathen hordes
Of ugly, foreign sand.

This photo is looking north, so that's Mauritania on the left and Mali to the right.

Very dry air makes the desert temperatures quite fickle, hot by day and surprisingly cool at night.

Sand Flows Soft and Easy

Rounded forms and yearning folds
Employ a lacework web
That beds old stones,
Cradles every stray acacia tree
And snugs our senses
In the softness of its sight.

Each day with faultless regularity,
The surfaces are raked and cleaned
By fingers of the wind,
Flamed in glosses of the sun,
Shadows draped across each thin declivity
Before the work is done.

And then when day submits to dusk
The moon ascends
To share its cool, pretended light
And dunes all sigh
And rest their silhouettes
Against the pale sky
Releasing faded warmth
To wander night like lonesome love
Departed from some rendezvous,
Waiting for the dawn above.

Unusual warmth one evening, along with a thin sliver of moon, made for
a perfect night.

Deep Velvet Night

Evening breeze turned warm and danced
In slow ellipses through the sugar light
And stirred old ghosts of bygone caravans
Until they wakened from their desert sleep
And spread for us a perfect nomad night.

The dark reached out in velvet gloves
Conducting unknown music up from earth
And placed a crescent moon into the sky
To mock the isolation of this place,
And orchestrate our wonder of rebirth.

Enclosed within the newfound womb
Attached by night's elastic black,
We felt the beating heart of all this land
And knew its labored journey from the past,
And knew that we could never give it back.

Photo of the Richat Crater taken from the Discovery 2 satellite on
November 8, 1984.

The Richat Crater

A bruising, near delusional descent
Concluded down upon the crater floor
Where three concentric rings
Roughcast a florid core
In mottled red and black
With not a trace of lava in the track.

The origin of its geology
Is full of argument and mystery.
Some think it gouged by heavy winds
That blew in a colossal whorl,
While others hold a different view,
Observing that this crater so distinct
Is carbon-dated back
To when the dinosaurs became extinct.

Advancing through that awful place,
Lurching over rock in lowest gear,
We chewed on this
And muttered darkly of apocalypse
As we resolved the case:
A meteor had walloped earth
And hit the bull's-eye here.

Ouadane

City walls tumble, sprawl, yet spine
The minaret erect, calling all to prayers
Beside the clutch of palms
That pool a pleasing green into serene
Soothing just behind the eyes,
Rare relief from burning skies.

Built nine centuries ago, it served
Great caravans that trundled through
Before they faced the desperate forty days
—As much in doubt as castaways—
To reach the legendary place southeast
Where gold and salt and slaves were due.

Those unforgiving routes lie buried now
And travelers long ago withdrew,
Until our curious group turns up
To wave at people in the street,
And then explain to skeptical police
The cockeyed nature of our feat.

Next day at dawn
Two hours of loud Quran began
—As if for infidels, no less would do—
Especially since we had materialized
From out of desolation scorned,
Arriving here from distant Timbuktu.

The police didn't believe we came from the east. But given our looks and the lack of a passport entry stamp from any normal route, they eventually shrugged and let us go.

This final episode caught the spirit of our whole adventure, as if it had been scripted.

Racing Time and Tide

It meant to end in glassy dunes,
Land confused to find the sea,
Our final day,
Distance figured carefully
To strike the coast by four o'clock,
Avoiding highest tide, the beach
Still firm and fairly wide,
Western sky billowed bright,
An hour's easy drive,
Perhaps a little more,
Straight down a sand-packed shore
Into the city where, our odyssey complete,
We'd celebrate the feat.

But lurking, not quite beaten,
Stuffed in ragged pockets
Laced with wiry filaments of grass,
The sand prepared its last-ditch stand
And we got stuck.
It fought the efforts of our crew,
Resisted everything we tried to do
And though the ocean lay
But one scant mile away,
The hours—helpless—fluttered by
From four to five and on past six,
The tide now rolling in
And soon the sun to set,
Our sweet arrival plans unmet.

And yet, and yet
In one perfected, further try,
Alberto willed it otherwise.
We burst those bounds and
Spitting sand shot free
Until at seven we hit the sea
Where Ali knelt and praised his god
And felt the liquid waves
He'd never seen before.

But time had near run out
And it remained to drive
The softened, fast-receding shore.
We never hesitated, took an action
Bordered on the barking mad,
And down that darkened coast we sped
As Hadji led, driving
With those demons at his heels
While ocean swells lapped up
To lick the wheels and jutting dunes
Pressed in upon our side.

We made it just as nighttime fell,
A foot of beach to spare
And one last slope to climb,
Exalting at this final ride
On finished sand and hollowed time
Between the teeth of hungry tide.

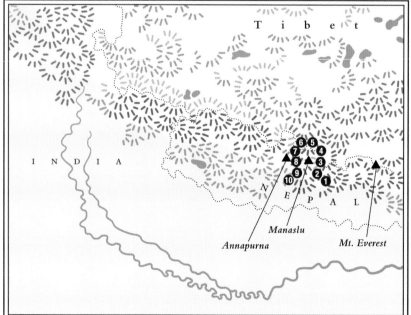

At our lunch stop the first day, Russ Osterman studies a map while Brad Nichols looks over his shoulder. Kelly Shannon and Kevin Hessee are on the right.

Russ waited for me at the top of Larkya La Pass. We rested for ten minutes before starting the steep descent.

The Long Trek around Manaslu

Seven of us had organized a month-long expedition into the Himalayas to circle Manaslu, the eighth highest mountain on earth. The trek began in lowlands Nepal, proceeded north past ever-higher peaks, and then turned west along the Tibetan border before descending through a river valley that separates the Manaslu massif from the Annapurna range. We started out with a good Sherpa guide, fifty porters, and high hopes.

By the time we finished, my altimeter watch showed our cumulative elevation gain—with much up and down—had reached 50,000 vertical feet. Unfortunately, a freak late season monsoon dumped 10 feet of snow on a key pass, and we encountered several tragedies along the way. An avalanche killed a German trekker one day ahead of us on the trail. Several days later, while climbing over the highest pass, we came upon the body of a dead monk shortly before dawn. Apparently he had died only a few hours earlier, trying to return to his homeland in Tibet.

One member of our group injured his knees on a grinding descent and had to turn back. The head Sherpa assigned two porters to help him walk out to the nearest village, where he caught a bus to Kathmandu and a flight home.

The sequence of ten poems included here follows our route faithfully, reflecting experiences and emotions—from valley to peak, including both exultation and tribulation. The map shows the route and locates Manaslu relative to Annapurna and Mount Everest.

Panorama

An afternoon ascending steps,
Massive stones worn smooth
By waves of smiling Nepalese
Each seeking truth atop this ridge
That holds their venerated monument,
And offers us our own awaited sight,
The Himalayas
Leaping over, slashing through the clouds,
A higher stationed sun
Unleashing them in brilliant light

To set our spirits free
Like hawks in thrall to distant peaks,
Intent to pierce their bones,
Lift out the marrow of this trek
That we'd be on for weeks
Across Nepal,
Along the border of Tibet,
Passes stiff with snow,
Fifty porters, seven of us,
Our Sherpa guide, no ceremony,
Simply that we go.

We reached the ridgetop, waved good-bye to Nepalese heading to a Hindu shrine, and saw—calling us from above the clouds—our home for the next month.

Down within the Green

The sweetest green on earth
Must be oases slipped between
Rapacious desert sands,
Or snow-fed fields that live beneath
Short-tempered mountain stands,
Gentle places juxtaposed
With harsh and brutal lands,
An existential fate . . .

And we swung off that
Panoramic high
Into a tide of oxen carts
And ambling villagers proceeding down
A happy path that fell away
Until it reached the valley far below,
Plumped and loved and sheathed
In softest layers, gently curved contours.

Its provenance was ages past,
And we imbibed the ripened air,
Drowsy in those scents of earth and ease,
The hum of whirring wings
And cultivated care.

Having spent the previous afternoon climbing, this morning we descended to a lush river bed below.

This wasn't the highest bridge we crossed, but it was the longest.

Suspension Bridges

Few structures
Hang together with the loose élan
Of high suspension bridges

Stretched in full consent
To yards of sway,
Rusty cables, elements of fray,

Open in design, gaping view
On flimsy footboards,
Patching overdue,

The river hissing like
An ill-fed chasm
Eager wild below,

Its eyes licking
Every step we take
On shaky knees, with vertigo.

The Route to Deng

Its black repute was well preserved
In oft-told tales that
Underscored the dark appeal of risk.
This route was loose and sheer and
Given newly saturated slopes,
Fresher menace overhung
The long established fear.

A newer bridge had washed away,
Its predecessor, looking rotten, sagged
And we were thunderstruck,
But stepped ahead, trusting luck
Until each foot was back on solid ground,
The trail climbing, snaking up around
Perverse convexities of rock
Shouldered out to chasm edge
Until the goddamn path just quit,
Narrowed to a chiseled ledge
Not quite a boot-length wide,
Our only choice to inch its face,
Encouraged by the guide.

And then came awful news
That up ahead an avalanche had spilled
In clots of rock and splintered trees,
The path wiped out,
A German trekker killed . . .
Our shell of boldness cracked,
Perhaps was even broken, yet
His time had come, not ours,
An instinct felt, though never spoken.

A late-season storm poured rain for two days, with
snow at higher levels, causing difficulties that would
seriously impact our trek.

We sorely wanted to stop at this village and stay awhile, but there were miles to go.

Samagaon

The day was fresh, eye-filling clear,
Our trail unruffled, cruising
At a middling height,
When we walked into Samagaon
And found ourselves charm struck
Within its medieval sight.

A woman sat outside her rustic home
Spinning on a patched-up loom,
Each thread caressed by sun,
As children perched on heavy walls
Releasing squeals
Like elfin arrows shot in fun.

Watching from a timbered balcony,
A lady slid her Mona Lisa smile our way
While combing long, jet-black hair,
And let the gesture in her eyes
Connect to every step we took,
Her perfect bosom bare.

Men stopped their work to stare at us,
Inquisitive while threshing grain,
And often waved an antique flail
To share this time, so briefly parallel,
As we continued up the trail.

First Sight of Manaslu

Our Sherpa guide stopped short
And shot us each a look
That seemed a little sly
And said "Manaslu" pointing
To the sky
And it was there,

Exceeding all that we expected,
Holding multi-towered tops so high
They seemed reflected
From some distant, cosmic world
Beamed here to taunt the earth-made clouds,

And we were captured, conquered,
Lifted up beyond mere thrill
And fused into that mountain's greater force,
Submitted to its stronger will,
Transformed into foot soldiers
Marching firmly on its noble course.

Not well known by Westerners, Manaslu is a magnificent, supremely remote mountain.

Larkya La Pass:
The Climb

We pitched our highest camp,
Tents staked out on beds of snow,
Four hours of fitful dreams
And then we had to go,
Start the climb at three,
Walking single file, moving silently
Immersed in bitter cold,
Enclosed in private thoughts—
This snow too deep,
No semblance of a trail,
The point of no return now passed,
Unthinkable to fail.

Our headlamps swayed
Expelling tiny shards of light
That jerked at crazy angles
Up into the moonless night
And time—antagonized—began
To rail against each crawling mile,
Bodies straining up the bleak defile,
No longer in a proper line,
Some of us behind,
Plodding slowly, slipping far apart
Inside those walls that echoed back
A solitary sound,
The pounding rhythm of my heart.

The pass is nearly 17,000 feet high, and a freakish level of snow made it more difficult than normal.

Footprints creased the lonely track
Where I must go
Like frozen orders signaled up
From buried land below,
And when at last the sun appeared
It came deprived of warmth,
But gifted me with vision,
Eyes intent to see the top,
The summit of this pass,
A trek mate waiting there
At seventeen thousand feet
Where trail would then begin to drop.

Eight unceasing hours spent
And still ahead the steep descent,
But first this wedge of time to stop,
Let go compression in my chest,
Muscles momentarily at rest,
Sit down surrendered to the ease
And watch the sun throw diamonds in the snow,
And drink the sky's triumphant blue,
Braced against each blast of wind,
Alive at every blow—
Seize these moments, precious few
Within the circled warrior peaks
And noble ice-wrapped walls,
To know again so dearly
Why such high adventure calls.

It felt great to reach the high point and start down, but the route quickly turned steep,
and softened ice made the six-hour descent somewhat dangerous.

Larkya La Pass:
Lying in the Snow

The man had died
Just hours ago this night,
Alone when cold turned grave
And he still traveling past the light,
His robes now fallen loose,
Felt boots upon his feet,
Returning to Tibet we learned,
His journey near complete.

He'd found a way across the pass
And almost down,
His face at peace, but clenched,
Not quite a frown,
A look released of former goals,
Intended miles to go,
This Buddhist monk now dead
Lying in the snow.

The dead man had been visiting in India, was returning home to Tibet,
and encountered the heavy snow in the pass.

Forest Magic

Like ice-melt loosened from
Some crystal pinnacle, we trickled down
Onto the ragged, lower slopes,
Before a necessary scramble
Over boulder-strewn moraine,
The final residue of rock and risk.

And then we entered forest
Filled with pointing spruce and pine,
The trees all angled up as if in prayer,
A sea of acolytes
Below those showy peaks,
And stands of rhododendron, rusty reds,
Mosses velvet yellow green
Soothing us with colors
In an earthy rich and aromatic scene.

A stream close by was full of bluster,
Leaping rocks with sounds of life and joy,
And suddenly we found ourselves
Full-throated in response,
Shouts and laughter exponentially increased,
Our days of stress and splendor
Locked in spring-tight tension
Suddenly released.

*We felt full-bodied, sensuous delight to be back
on real earth again.*

We had come full circle. It was a month later now, and harvest time.

At Harvest Time

The river ran insistent, born and bred
To cleave the deep, unerring gorge
That separates majestic Manaslu
From summits of the Annapurna range,
A busy, twisting stream that opened up
The land to consequential change.

The trail descended, loping down
Through folds of worthy land, where nature
Wrestled ridges into softer sights,
And terraced legacies of efforts past
Eased into the view,
And took no notice as our boots
Came tramping, tramping through.

We relished quiet villages,
Our taste for chaos cast aside,
Replaced by rice and sorghum, wheat,
Families working underneath the sun,
Haystacks framed in autumn rhythms
Centuries ago begun.

Mountains fell away and hills reclined,
The miles slipping off our backs
Within those yellowed, ceaseless days
Returning us to soft, remembered lives
Pulled down from distant shelves,
The strumming flights transported home,
And struggle fitting into former selves.

Boab trees strore water in their jug-like trunks during monsoon season. It lasts them through the long, fiercely dry period, when they also shed leaves to conserve water and energy.

About fifty groups participated at a Sing-Sing in Papua New Guinea in 2006 when I was there.

Outback Down Under

ON A BUSINESS TRIP in the late 1980s, I took a weekend and flew from Sydney, Australia to Ayers Rock to see this largest single piece of rock on earth. It rises 1,000 feet above dead flat desert and is more than 2 miles long. Although a surprise rainstorm kept me from climbing it, an Aboriginal guide took me on a fascinating walk around the perimeter, explaining every notch and furrow. They call the place Uluru and it is sacred for them. Nearby there is a smaller but equally bizarre rock outcropping called the Olgas.

Several years later, after retiring, I had time for fuller adventures, including travel to what the Aussies call the Top End. My first goal was Kakadu Park, located beside the Aboriginal preserve known as Arnhem Land, a region of wild diversity, including the largest saltwater crocodiles. Next on my list was the Kimberley, a nearly inaccessible region in the northwest bounded by the Timor Sea and the Indian Ocean. Due to monsoons, its climate alternates between extremes, partly tropical and partly desert. On both adventures I was the one old guy, and a Yank at that, mixed in with Aussies, Europeans, and Japanese mostly in their twenties. They more or less adopted me.

We bumped over dirt roads and enjoyed hiking and swimming. When it got dark, we'd find a decent place to camp and fix dinner. Arrangements were basic. Sleeping bags on the ground, mosquito netting strung from trees over the whole spread, anchored on the corners by rocks.

Two generations ago, people along the Sepik River and in the highlands of Papua New Guinea were still living as headhunters and cannibals, in some ways not unlike their Stone Age ancestors. To help change those habits, the government started an annual event called a Sing-Sing, during which tribal groups compete fiercely for prize money based on costumes and activities. It was a fascinating spectacle, but for our small group, visits with Huli Wigmen in the highlands and trips upriver to see villagers in the lowlands proved to be even more interesting.

Uluru and the Olgas

Dawn arrives to greet the earth
And opens sky to blue, while Uluru
Rises in its daily birth, blazing orange
Illuminating creases,
Sacred furrows formed in stone
Like Lilliputian lines designed
To strap and hold, preclude the further
Levitation of this monolithic block,
Largest ever earthly surfaced
Singularity of rock.

And not so far away
Across the dry electric distance
Supercharged by day
And filled with brooding currents of the night,
The eerie Olgas glow,
Mutant rocks ten stories high
That rear each odd, misshapen head
In purple opulence and red
To dazzle like some rough-cut jewel
Set into the belly of an aging land
Turned wanton, naked, cruel.

At both dawn and dusk, the rock becomes alive, radiating energy in electric colors.

Geologists explain these mountains as stripes of black lichen over orange silica, layered onto bands of sandstone.

The Bungle Bungles

The old recumbent mountain range
Held thousands of outlandish humps and hills
Confusing and amazing
Clad in tiger stripes intensely blazing.
Rounded pinnacles were everywhere,
A vast encampment crammed
With giant cones and swirled towers,
Pumpkin houses five to fifty stories tall,
Coffee-colored crackle banding all.

Water filled each billabong
And greened the ghost gum trees
That parch through months of dire need,
Then have to cope until deep floods recede.
Like boab trees and Aboriginals
They meet these flip-flops of reality
With apt, inventive practicality;

And we enthused about the mountain's look,
Likened it to art, fauvist in design,
Inspired, expressive work,
Wonderfully extreme,

Leaving me to ponder life and art:
Less the issue which comes first,
Than our accepted structures of esteem.

Written in the Rock

It is written in the rock,
This grudging epic of ordeal,
Age and wither, weariness,
Defective edges bearing witness,
Troubles still—the Wet against the Dry,
Clouds hurling huge monsoons
That drown the land for months
As jagged flashes streak the sky
Until the Wet, spent, is seared, sucked
Back into the desert Dry.

Cracked and flayed,
Weakened by ill wind
The land slumbers, dying silently,
Tired for all eternity,
Indifferent to the meager trees,
Serpents underneath, mammals
Holding young in pouches, on the run,
As well as black and gray matte-finished men
Who treasure every "walkabout"
Beneath this iron-fisted sun;

Who live confluent with all creatures,
Every animal and plant,
Each peak and gully, trees
And termite mounds,
Broad gaps as well as close proximities,
The wholeness of the ground
Imbibe it all they do,
Become as one with floods,
And then configure to the Dry,

Defeating force by acquiescence,
Bending into being,
Settled into near transparency
And trusting what they're seeing,
Every element a wonder
Drummed beneath their feet,
Measured up into their eyes,
Passed into their stories,
Sung into their song,

Each presence registered
With pictures written in the rock
Speaking out in yellows,
Rusty red and ocher, chalky white,
Due respect for every hero—
Lightning Man and Turtle, Kangaroo,
The Birds in flight
And Woman given godlike to creation.
Spirits of these things they know,
Etched to catch millennia flown past

And stream a future meant to last,
That centers simply on what is,
No idiom for rich,
Nor meaning meant for poor,
Embedded now for fifty thousand years,
Of never less, nor more.

The cycle from dry to wet season each year is violent in the extreme.

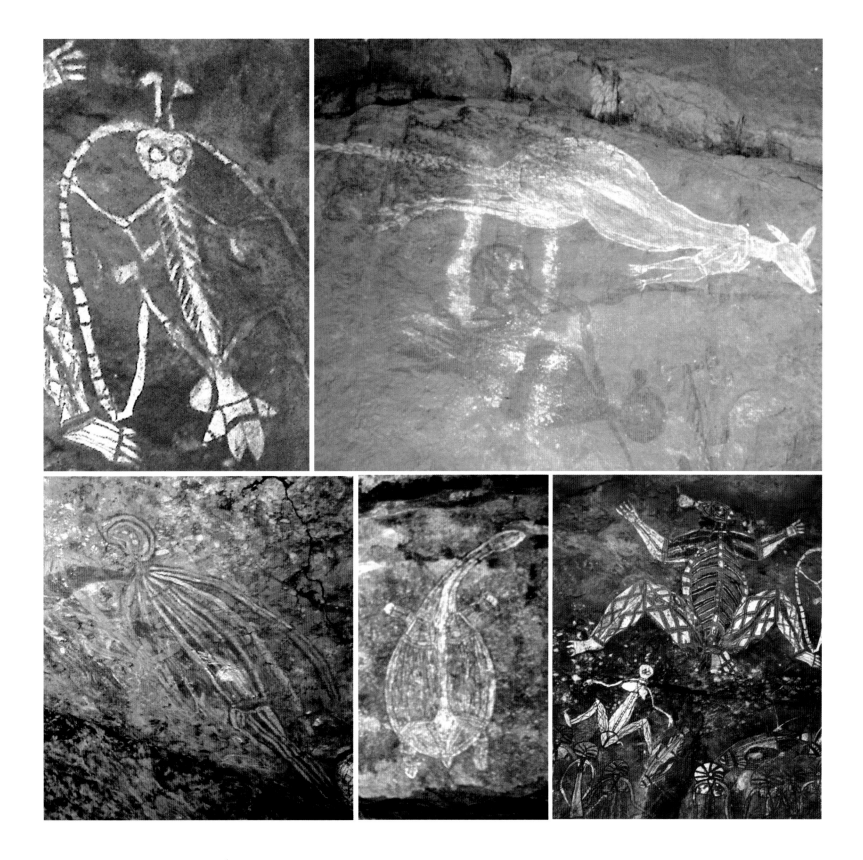

I've managed to get myself hung out to dry a number of times, but this was the worst.

Return from Jim Jim Falls

Threads of fear
Knit their menace tight across
My chest, tied a knot
Into my brain . . .

 I was lost.

In temperature about a hundred five
With precious little shade,
And not content to wait
Until our group was geared to go,
I'd gotten good direction from the guide
And started my return alone
Across that high and wild plateau.

I'd gone perhaps a couple miles
Hammered by the heat, walking dazed
Inside some inner space,
My thoughts untethered, loose and stupid
In that hard, unbounded place
Until the moment when I suddenly
 Came clear
Confused by look-alike terrain
Notorious for deadly snakes
And felt that blanket wrap of fear.

Climbing up a rock outcrop,
I shouted hard and listened harder,
Hearing only hissing wind
And asked myself again
With every expletive I knew
Where in hell my mind had been.

Returning yet another quarter mile,
I braced and firmed myself
In patchy shade falling off a tree
And yelled far more aggressively,
Hoping, straining for response,
But only silence answered me.

Two minutes wet with sweat went by
Before I knew I had to move,
Was seriously off route,
The group would never hear,
And walking back ten minutes more
Beneath that incandescent sun
I climbed a higher slope and roared
With all the force of surging, sick concern
And heard—by god it was—
A faintest, weakest wisp
Of audible return.

For me it was a clarion call,
A trumpet blast that blew its golden note
Into the sprockets of my spine
Though, to be sure, forty fewer steps
Or thirty seconds more, who knows
What fate was mine.

Homing in upon that sound
I scrambled forward full of sweet relief,
Yet gave each step accentuated care,
Not wanting some horrific snake
To strike at my salvation there.

Huli Wigmen

Feathered Huli,
Works of bold intimidation
Flaunting wigs of human hair
Across the tension-ravaged air,
Knife their yellowed faces
Deep into our thin facade
With every Stone Age stare.

They dance the troubled history
Of pure revenge,
That registry of hunted heads
Rolled into a constancy of fears—
An arrow flash, a sudden start,
No shield a shield for warring heart,
No breath nor step secure,
No life apart.

Descended here
Beyond that bleak imperium
Devised in symmetry of settled scores,
They beat their drums
And wave well-sharpened spears
That once sought flesh in flight,
Groomed exactly as before,
But aiming now no more than sight.

Imagine meeting them when they were on a head-hunting raid, only a generation or two ago.

Sepik River Spirits

Rich and thickened waters in collusion flow,
Ingesting mountain residue
To feed the green violence of growth.
Birds of paradise perch in trees
And singe limbs with multi-flaming hues
While long canoes
Cut creases lapping onto riverbanks.

Village people smile and spread displays
Of axe and drum and gruesome mask,
Each mordant figure carved
Into the scowl of prior days,
That time of severed heads and hurled spears,
Transfigured harvest, former fears.

And enemy conspiracies still fuel
Phantom fire within each spirit house,
Vengeance permeating thatch and weave,
A sorcery to settle debts,
Resolve the needs of those who grieve,
And leave invisible remains
On skull-like bowls once filled
With boiling human brains.

Intruding here, uneasy in our steps,
We contemplate anew
The broth that's nourished all our days
With flavors dark, familiar, rich
And swimming full, no doubt, of butchered bits
Long appetizing to our ways.

Villagers along the river greeted us with smiles and dances,
but their spirit houses felt vaguely foreboding inside.

The Nature of Experience

EIGHT POEMS selected here share a philosophy. They express it from five different corners of the world—including serious mountains and a Japanese zen garden—but the thought is the same.

These journeys begin in a gathering storm, where I hurried down a hillside in the Andes, leaning hard against a wind that mocked me with its vitality. Next we stand at Monument Valley in Arizona beneath buttes, towers, and spires that scream their defiance at the forces of erosion. Then we twist through a slot canyon that elevates the force of nature into art. A ten-day trek around Mont Blanc climbs over passes from France to Italy and on to Switzerland, and verifies the debt that pleasure owes to pain.

While still in the Alps, but under the Eiger, we look at the inner need for challenge, accepting—often embracing—the dark appeal of risk. And in "To Rise or Fall," set in the grandeur of the Karakoram Mountains, I've sharpened this theme into primal questions, not just for travel and adventure, but for life itself.

The final two poems, which recount my experiences climbing a small peak in Patagonia and gazing down into the famous Ryoanji Garden in Kyoto, Japan, recognize chance and opportunity, and the abiding benefits of optimism. One poem reflects these in terms of the past, the other looks forward. Both appreciate that life is an odyssey and that, at its core, there is but one imperative—to live it. To truly live it.

Seeing the strength and anger in that sky was worth the worry.

Old Alliances

Upon a gray and sullen sky, three gulls
Inscribed hard angles of their flight
While I began to hurry down
A hill affording me the truer sight
And saw dark columns of a rain
Make fast alliance with approaching night.

Leaning hard against the wind
Now mocking me with its vitality,
I thought again of time and flow,
This turn of new reality, and laughed,
Recalling memories of youth,
Its fresh-eyed absence of mortality.

Monument Valley

Aching time and silence
Steal the innocence of open space,
Where sly possession of emaciated air
Empowers orphaned monuments
To clarify their presence here.

Castellated towers, solitary buttes,
Even fearful spires,
Some as thin as desert apparitions,
Bare their hard remembrance
Scornful of the fossil waters, older epochs
Of unspeakable discontinuity
That carried off their world.

Like angry gods
Decapitated long ago,
Then dragged beneath a shallow desert sea
Turned up by time,
They flaunt their perpendicularity
And shriek
In flaming changing colors
That they live.

The poem barely touches the wonder of this vista.

Sonata in a Slot Canyon

Washed whorled rock flows composed
Embracing quirk and crimp,
Arranged so convolutions polished bright
Ignite upward
Scored into inverted consequence.

The channeled scintillations
Orchestrate our muted steps,
Squeezed to fit confounding twists,
While framing up much larger meaning—
Try to loosen truly,
Curl and glide,
But heed the deities that wink and hide
Inside the skew of moving course,
Observe how floods resolve:
Abrasion, absolution, and evolve.

For even flights of stone
Extol more than force alone,
Inspired higher,
Lofted from a many-chambered heart
Imagined into art.

*This little slot canyon, close to my home, reinspires
me every time I walk through it.*

Around Mont Blanc

September slid its sunbeams
Down through vintage sky,
An aftertaste of summer's warmth
That sparkled in the champagne light;
And we walked high above the valley floor
Thrilled by ridges, sculpted peaks,
That famous summit dome
Flanked by snowfields silver bright,
With glacial cleavage all on show,
While russet rooftops far below
Flecked the forest green
Into a pleasing pastel sight
That promised lodging for the night.

We had but four such golden days
To usher in our trek around Mont Blanc,
And then October came to stack thick clouds,
Produce a breezy ambiguity,
The prelude to an ambush waiting
On the Col du Reigne,
The classic pass from France to Italy
That welcomed us with biting sleet.
So we descended once again
And found a cozy inn
Complete with dinner, wine, and cheese,
Stories ripe with laughter, downy quilts
And little thought of what was coming after.

We started late in the season on our trek around Mont Blanc, pushing luck, and were punished (rewarded?) accordingly.

That early storm
Was just a small discomfort,
Merely finger food, hors d'eouvre
Compared to heavy banquet served
Crossing through to Switzerland
Where we were swallowed up in white,
A blizzard full of fury
Straight into the face, visability obscured,
This gentle trek slammed into a race
For safety down below.

Thereafter, gods of cold caprice
Abandoned us to shifting fate,
Allowed some hidden pendulum to alternate,
Granting quite extraordinary vistas
Stretched beneath a friendly sun,
Then striking with its cold and snow or rain,
Beauty marbled through with pain.

In retrospect, the only constant was
Unfailing camaraderie
And also—now that time has dulled
Both misery and fear—
We learned it is travail,
Even more than treat, that gives
The oddly pleasing taste to bittersweet.

Our guide was quite worried, more than we were, but then, she knew more than we knew.

Under the Eiger

Reclining on a meadow ridge,
I locked my gaze
Onto the Eiger's massive wall,
The one carved sheer
That offers climbers there
A hundred famous ways to fall.

And I perceived
The Eiger holds its breath
To stay so rigid, daunting, firm
For humans philosophically disposed
To dangle, squirm,
Defying death,
Rejecting gravity and storm,
As measure of their courage,
Confirmation of their form.

Festooned with rope and useful gear
To manage ice, defeat the cold,
Avoid a slide, control their fear,
Courageous climbers come . . .
And sure enough from time to time,
As if by mutual consent,
The Eiger all at once exhales
And murders some.

At the hotel beneath the Eiger's wall there is a brisk business, complete with viewing deck and telescopes, of guests watching climbers court death.

To Rise or Fall

Crystal palaces of rock and ice,
Those purest flourishes of mountain music
Strike the bright, ironic chords
That sing their surgery into my bones,
Impelling limbs to climb,
To scale intentions of the mind
Possessed by keen believing
Out beyond the vex of gravity
That grounds our fragile act of being.

Higher up, heads get lighter,
Drift into a less connected state
Where naked circumstance
Will proposition fate,
Where moves metastasize, each choice
The choice that owns posterity,
That gives away recourse,
Its knife-edge honed
Into those primal either / or's . . .
To quit or try, to rise or fall, to live
        Or simply die.

In Hollywood they say "cut to the chase." In business we called it "the bottom line."

The Summit of Cerro Cristal

Patagonian grasses never flinched,
Just shifted angles
Crawling up the slopes
Like caterpillars twitching green,
While beech trees, bent and huddled,
Flexed against the gravity
And threw indifferent shade,
A place to pause and watch the condors
Fly their high redundant loops.

Too soon, however,
Trees and grasses simply quit,
Leaving only rubble rock, the wind
And eight of us
To labor up the steep incline,
Eventually to find a crimp
Of flattened land
Crouching there above the timberline.

It offered level footing
And a floor-to-ceiling view.
We could have stopped right there!
Lago Argentino spread below
Its waters silted milky blue,
A glacier calving columns of ice,
The Andes draped in early snow.

But Cerro Cristal's summit
It was not, so we set out again
On nasty scree, where three steps up
Saw two come down, and wind
Turned vicious with abusive gusts
That swung from side to side
Upsetting rudiments of balance,
Danger of a nasty slide.

At the top our talk defaulted to
The usual points—spirit and resolve,
Satisfaction climbing strong—
Although the sun was now in clouds
And wind had raked the summit bleak,
And we did not stay long.

A fast descent brought hot debate:
What difference did the summit make?
Diminishing returns, some said,
Risk and suffering for just a minor peak,
A trifling increment of extra view.

All that is true, quite true, and yet
When I reflect on life's quick run
Of pleasure and regret,
It was the actions taken whole
That stretched into a life I won't forget.

I remember a wise man saying, "The beauty is in the chase," although I didn't believe him at the time.

A Garden in Kyoto

Petals fall from rosy circumstance.
My old and crinkled being
Sailing down upon uncertain seas,
Steering less with either eye
Than by an inner seeing,
Floating over fine-grained swells
Until the crash and thunder
Dark devised as rock.

I climb its rearing, creviced shape
Exploring caves that deepen
Into soft serenity,
Yet find I cannot stay,
Urgencies unspent pull me away,

Revolved again
Into accrued and musing odyssey
With new felicity of sight,
To seek another place
As crystal hard,
But lacquered open to the light.

This, too, is a waiting and necessary sight.

Maps with Poem Locations

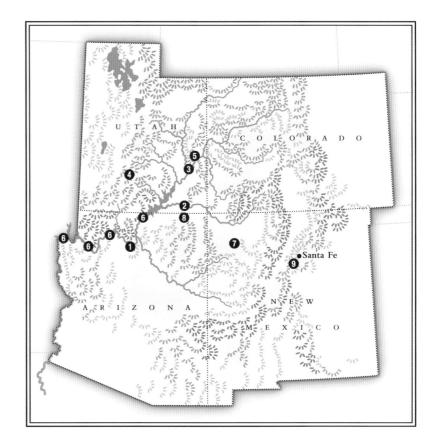

Countries in the order of their appearance

Kenya	Pakistan
Peru	Chile
Botswana	Italy
Cambodia	Namibia
Mauritania	Ecuador
Venezuela	New Zealand
Brazil	Ethiopia
Galapagos Islands	Ireland
Tanzania	Argentina
Mali	Australia
China	Myanmar
Tibet	Syria
Nepal	Jordan
Switzerland	Croatia
Japan	Greece
Egypt	Uzbekistan
India	Papua New Guinea
United States	France

Poems Located in the United States

1. *Late Light Falling into Grand Canyon*
2. *Null Hypothesis at Muley Point*
3. *Incendiary*
4. *Hoodoos at the Dance*
5. *Patience*
6. *Down the Colorado River*
7. *Chaco Canyon*
8. *Monument Valley*
9. *Sonata in a Slot Canyon*

Poems Located in Africa

1. *Climbing Kilimanjaro*
2. *Leopard at Dusk*
3. *Honeyed Desert Dunes*
4. *Reporting on the Wildebeest*
5. *Dogon Dancers*
6. *Pyramid*
7. *Timbuktu*
8. *Desert Spaces*
9. *Desert Never Meant to Be*
10. *Father of All Dunes*
11. *Colony at the Cape*
12. *Empty Peeled*
13. *The Solitary Maasai*
14. *Cheetah Rap*
15. *Etched*
16. *Night Sounds on the Serengeti*
17. *Mursi Woman*
18. *Ethiopian Gothic*
19. *Rock-Hewn Churches of Lalibela*
20. *Dreams along the Nile*
21. *The Ruins at Luxor*
22. *The Ultimate Sahara Expedition*

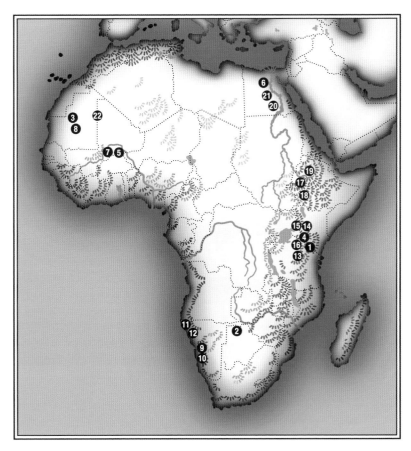

Poems Located in South America

1. *Machu Picchu in the Twilight*
2. *Angel Falls*
3. *The Amazon: Imposing Order*
4. *Straight Talk in the Galapagos*
5. *Patagonia*
6. *The "Lost World"*
7. *Jungle Depths*
8. *Tierra del Fuego*
9. *An Advancing Glacier*
10. *Old Alliances*
11. *The Summit of Cerro Cristal*

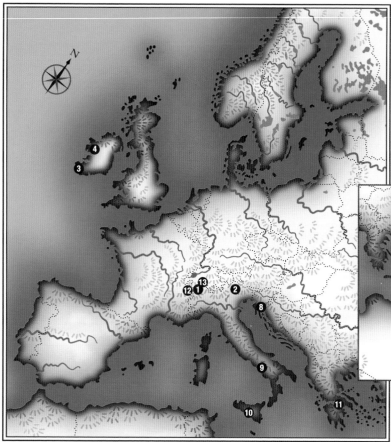

Poems Located in Europe and the Middle East

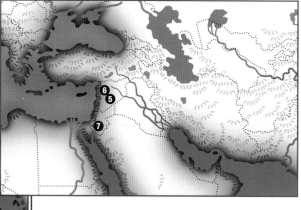

1. The Matterhorn
2. Musings in the Dolomites
3. The Irish Coast
4. Connemara
5. Palmyra
6. St. Simeon's Pillar
7. Petra
8. The Maximus of Must
9. Pompeii
10. Pale Temple
11 To Find the Parthenon
12 Around Mont Blanc
13 Under the Eiger

Poems Located in Australia, New Zealand, and Papua New Guinea

1. Pure Primeval
2. The Southern Cross
3. Uluru and the Olgas
4. The Bungle Bungles
5. Written in the Rock
6. Return from Jim Jim Falls
7. Huli Wigmen
8 Sepik River Spirits

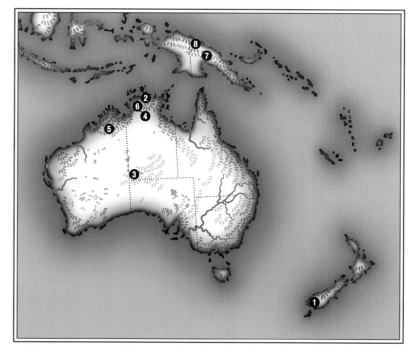

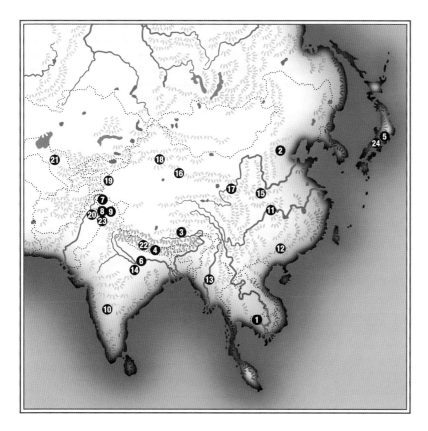

Poems Located in Asia

1. *Angkor*
2. *This Great Wall*
3. *Lhasa*
4. *Mount Everest from Tengboche*
5. *Good Morning, Fuji*
6. *River Ganges at Benares*
7. *The Karakoram Highway*
8. *The Baltoro Glacier and K2*
9. *Concordia and the Moon*
10. *Sky Clad People*
11. *Yangtze Gorges*
12. *Beside the River Li*
13. *The Kingdom of Bagan*
14. *Temples of Khajuraho*
15. *The Emperor's Last Campaign*
16. *Dunhuang*
17. *Buddha by the River*
18. *Jiaohe Was Its Name*
19. *Kashgar and Its Sunday Market*
20. *Hunza*
21. *Samarkand*
22. *The Long Trek around Manaslu*
23. *To Rise or Fall*
24. *A Garden in Kyoto*

pg. 1: This caravan emerged from the violet haze of a sandstorm between Timbuktu and the Taoudenni salt mine, in Mali.

pg. 2: Paiju Peak thrusts above the Baltoro Glacier in the Karakoram Mountains.

pg. 3: Sahara sand dunes roll all the way to the sea in Mauritania.

Sunstone books may be purchased for educational, business, or sales promotional use. For information please write: Special Markets Department, Sunstone Press, P.O. Box 2321, Santa Fe, New Mexico 87504-2321.

Project and Editorial Director: Joanna Hurley, HurleyMedia LLC
Design and Production: David Skolkin / Skolkin + Chickey
Printed in China

Library of Congress Cataloging-in-Publication Data available from the publisher upon request.

Photographic Credits

Friends traveling with me:
Pages 39, 74, 77 (top), 96, 149: Carol Williamette
42: Janet Russo, Bellevue Productions
46: (left); 73: Brad Nichols
52, 55, 56: Paul Whistler
59: Jack Johnson
117: Judy Haden
140 (bottom): Hank Hamlin
161: Russ Osterman
187: Ken Brown

Professional Photographers:
Page 14: John Warburton-Lee/Danita Delimont
18, 48, 185: Galen Rowell/Mountain Light

25, 136: Loren McIntyre/Scott McIntyre
26, 27: Tui De Roy/Roving Tortoise Photos
28: Ralph Bendjebar/Danita Delimont
29: Sneh Shah/Sneh Shah Photography
33 (lower): Kazuyoshi Nomachi/Galileo Picture Services
34: Richard l'Anson/Getty Images
35: (right) stock photo
58: Jon Arnold/Danita Delimont
103: Marcello Beccaceci/Southworld
105: (unknown photographer)
123: Peter Langer/Danita Delimont
150 (lower): (Richat Crater, satellite photo)
170: Gavriel Jecan/Danita Delimont

Maps by Deborah Reade, Santa Fe

Published in Santa Fe

WWW.SUNSTONEPRESS.COM
SUNSTONE PRESS/POST OFFICE BOX 2321/SANTA FE, NM 87504-2321/USA
(505) 988-4418/ORDERS ONLY (800) 243-5644/FAX (505)988-1025